The
Greatest
Among
You

A Student's
Guide to
Servant Leadership

Randy Sims

WORLDVIEW PRESS

THE GREATEST AMONG YOU
REVISED EDITION WITH STUDY GUIDE
Published by Worldview Press

Copyright © 2002 by A.R. Sims, Jr.

ISBN: 0-9720890-1-2

For information:

Worldview Press
P.O. Box 310106
New Braunfels, Texas 78131
Phone 830.620.5203
Fax 830.643.0217
www.worldview.org

cover and interior design by Jeff Stoddard
Study Guide contributor: Kelli Stuart

The Greatest Among You

A Student's Guide to Servant Leadership

To Amy, my love, my best friend,
my cheerleader, my soulmate.
To my children, Bryan, Stacy, Travis, and Gracie.
May servant leadership be your life's vision.
And to Jesus Christ, the
Captain of my soul.

Acknowledgements

William James once wrote, "Wherever you are it is your own friends who make your world." *The Greatest Among You* is a work drawn from the rich well of friends I have been blessed to know. This book is a result of paying attention in life's classroom and frequently raising my hand to ask questions of the Teacher, the Holy Spirit. He has allowed me many skilled tutors who have revealed to me the simplicity and beauty of a life of servant leadership. To all of them, named or not, I am forever in debt and grateful and without whom this book would be fruitless.

To my teammates, Todd Kent, Bill Jack, and Jeff Baldwin, who have expanded my worldview and challenged, encouraged, and cajoled me to turn random thoughts into a coherent presentation. Your lives are my leadership textbook.

To my parents, who exemplified the meaning of service through lives joined together for the purpose of giving them away for others.

To Joe White, Johnny Polk, Wes Neal, Nelson Cook, Larry Kramer, and Dave Simmons for having the patience to allow me to molt and develop wings. You have shown me the x's and o's of leadership.

To Bill Moore, Randy Allen, and Tom Nelson for holding the door of God's kingdom open that I might walk through.

To my good friends Kirk McJunkin, Scott Forester, Marty Secord, Larry Blake, Ron Miller, Mike Reppert, Fouad Faris, Keith Allred, Russ Pennell, Mike Goddard, Kenny Keller, Greg Wright, Luke and Lee Ellen Speckman, Kevin Harlan, Larry Hill, Vance Morris, Jeff Turpin, Tracy Tucker, Gary Jacobs, Mark Gregston, Royce Smith, Keith Myer, Don Talley, Kelly Boyd, Toby Stolhandske, Rick Nelson, David Bruns, Mark Wells, Mark Dudley, Marvin Smith, Matt Payne, Wes Sutton, and those of you who know your name should be here. Your lives have filled my pallet with the colors of friendship and fellowship that allowed me to paint this portrait of a leader.

To the Brothers Jeff: Baldwin and Stoddard. Your skilled work on this project has turned toilet paper into parchment.

To Kelli Stuart for her diligent labor in preparing a study guide that is not only useful and challenging but also full of fresh insights into God's book of leadership.

To the men and women of Kanakuk Kamps, Fellowship of Christian Athletes, T Bar M Sports Camp, Worldview Academy, Fellowship Bible Church, Oakwood Baptist Church, and Christ Presbyterian Church, laboring by your side has taught me the beat of a servant's heart.

To Tim Dunn, Doug Kieswetter, David Strassner, Randy King, Larry Cochran, and Andy Read, the faithful brothers who have supported Worldview Academy in presenting servant leadership to the students of America.

About the Author

Randy Sims is the executive director of Worldview Academy Ministries. He has trained Christian young people and adults in camps and ministries for over 20 years. He has served as a leadership staff member with Kanakuk Kamps, The Institute for Athletic Perfection, Fellowship of Christian Athletes national staff and T Bar M Sports Camp. As director of Worldview Academy Leadership Camps, Randy is responsible for the leadership training of over 2500 students and adults each year. Randy's work has afforded him the opportunity to lead chapel services for both college and professional sports teams, and to participate with the Billy Graham Crusade as a platform speaker. Randy lives with his wife, Amy, and their four children in Texas.

Worldview Academy is a non-denominational Christian camping, conference and resource ministry committed to helping Christians think and live in accord with their worldview so they may serve

Christ and lead the culture. Toward this end, WVA offers week-long leadership camps nation-wide—everywhere from Washington state to Virginia—for students 13 and older.

Although most other programs treat students like "fun-junkies," Worldview Academy treats students like real people who wrestle with tough issues. Students at WVA Leadership Camp spend about 26 hours in class, learning to "take captive every thought to make it obedient to Christ" (2 Cor. 10:5) They graduate with a basic understanding of non-Christian worldviews like the New Age movement and Islam, and the ability to apply the Christian worldview to fundamental questions about origins, aesthetics and human nature.

Classes integrate to form a foundation in three key areas: worldviews, apologetics/evangelism, and servant leadership. In addition, students apply what they've learned in various practicums, so that they leave the camp with both head-knowledge and heart-knowledge.

For more information about Worldview Academy programs and resources or to receive a leadership camp brochure, call 800.241.1123 or visit the website at www.worldview.org.

Let no one look down on your
youthfulness, but rather in speech, conduct, love, faith and purity,
show yourself an example of those who believe. 1 Timothy 4:12

Introduction

If you stacked all the books written on leadership and stood on the summit, you could see next week's weather forming in the distance. Each year, people spend millions for a myriad of leadership books, seminars, tapes, retreats, schools, degrees, gurus, etc. There are formulas, top ten lists, 7, 10, 12 habits, and secrets of leadership.

Enumerating leadership skills, character qualities, strategies, and development is not a difficult task. Most resources on leadership are a collection of the same points renumbered, reorganized, and reworded. When one boils down the essence of just what leadership is, one finds that the same main elements continue to come to the top of the kettle. If only these elements could be condensed, down to the blocking and tackling of the leadership craft. Now *that* would be something useful: *Cliff's Notes* on Leadership!

But almost every book or program speaks to those who are already in leadership positions. What about those who are preparing for leadership? In this age of information, where tools are lying about everywhere, it would seem that a student who desired to prepare for leadership would be able to find the needed materials for that goal. Unfortunately, that isn't the case. I searched for materials that boiled down these concepts of leadership for the student and found none. The following book seeks to fill that void—to help students understand the foundational principles in preparing for leadership.

If you say you want to be a leader, to be different and make a difference in your culture—if you have a desire to challenge others to a higher ideal and goal—this is where you will begin your quest. You will learn the elements of leadership: those concepts you need to understand in order to prepare yourself for a lifetime of leadership. We will discuss strategic, not tactical, leadership principles. Tactical principles are those detailed actions in leadership such as how to deal with different personality types, what career path should you take, or the *how to's* of day-to-day direction of a team. We will look at examples of the various principles but only for the sake of illustration. The details of leadership are up to you, your team, and God. Strategic leadership is the big picture: the wide angle shot as opposed to the close-up.

It is important to recognize a vital thread shuttling through the tapestry of *The Greatest Among You*. It is the call to servanthood. In Luke 22:26, Jesus is teaching His team during the last supper. The disciples have been arguing as to which one of them was the greatest. In what must have been a disappointed tone of voice, Jesus relates to them the hierarchy of His kingdom. Jesus says, "But it is not this way with you [the manner in which the earthly rulers lead by power and harshness], but the one who is the greatest among you must become like the youngest, and leader like the servant." In this Jesus taught all of us an important leadership lesson. Those who serve, lead, and those who lead, serve.

This principle of leadership is universal in that anyone of any faith can exercise it. Islam is one of the fastest growing worldviews in America. Led by the Nation of Islam, the religion is gaining footholds primarily in low-income, urban neighborhoods. The reason for this is that members of the Nation of Islam enter an urban neighborhood and clean up the streets of trash, debris, drugs, and gangs. They paint houses, plant flowers, replace broken windows and doors, and deploy security patrols. Having served the community, they then lead. And their leadership is enthusiastically followed by those they have served.

That the principle is universal does not make it less biblical. Actually, most biblical principles will work for the non-christian as well as the Christian. Adherence to the marriage covenant, loving others as you love yourself, personal responsibility, justice, and integrity are all biblical truths that may be applied by anyone. However, this discussion will be from a distinctly Christian perspective. We will draw conclusions based upon God's Word. These conclusions will only have meaning and permanence to the degree in which they align with Scripture. His Word is the straight edge to measure anything you read in this book or any other. I encourage you to question these principles, scrutinize the conclusions, and research the findings. Truth merits inspection, and if the concepts contained in this book are true, they will hold up under scrutiny. The principles that you will learn in this book are not new but rather timeless. They are timeless not because they work, but because they are true. Anyone can apply these principles and find some degree of success, but to experience eternal and lasting results, a commitment to Jesus Christ is essential.

In preparing for anything, steps must be taken to ensure success down the road. Recently, my son Bryan and I took a three-day camping trip in Colorado. To get ready for the three days, we spent three weeks gathering gear, studying trail maps, and planning meals. Preparation was essential. As much effort went into the preparation as into the actual trip. The same holds true in preparing for leadership. In order to see positive results in your future leadership, you must spend as much (if not more) time and effort in the groundwork of leadership.

As you can see in the diagram (figure 1), we will be constructing a building that will be an edifice representing a complete leader. We will build a foundation that will support the five pillars of leadership upon which rests the capstone of you as leader. Each chapter will add to the formation of the qualities you will need as you develop as a leader. Beginning with essential core concepts in leadership, we will continue on through the five pillars that support your desire to be a leader.

However, the most important step in any journey is the first one. It sets the direction you will follow for the second and one thousandth step. It is also critical because error increases with distance. If you have not taken the right step at the start, that misstep will be multiplied the more you travel. So with this in mind, let us take the first step in the right direction: a step toward a long and victorious journey of influence that begins with preparing for leadership.

figure 1

The Main Thing

*"All the kings in history
sent their people out to die for them.
There is only one king I know who decided
to die for his people."[1]
—Chuck Colson*

*"True greatness, true leadership,
is achieved not by reducing men to one's
service but in giving oneself in selfless
service to them."[2]
— J. Oswald Sanders*

A LEADER

CHRIST-LIKENESS

The main thing is to
keep the main thing the main thing.

I don't know who first said it (I first heard it from a friend, Keith Chancey), but this little axiom represents a lot of truth. It is vital in life and leadership to maintain perspective. Of course, the key to this statement is the identity of the main thing. I say identity because for the Christian the main thing is a person and your relationship with Him. What or who is your main thing?

In his book, *Half Time*, Bob Buford relates the story of an identity crisis in the Coca-Cola Corporation. Coke had just experienced one of the worst marketing disasters in American corporate history. Someone in the company had the brilliant idea of changing the formula of the soft drink to one that he believed tasted better. The resulting market confusion and outright anger among customers was enormous. In an effort to further dominate the soft drink market, Coke had made a critical misjudgment. Now the focus was how to re-establish their market position. A friend of

Buford's was called in to consult with the company's executives and help them formulate a strategy to regain dominance. At their first meeting, the consultant listened to the corporate officers pass blame around the room, express desire to fix the mistake, and make individual plans to move ahead. Finally, Buford's friend made his presentation. He placed a box in the middle of the expansive board room conference table and asked the executives, "What is in the box?" With puzzled looks on their faces, they glanced around the room to see if anyone else knew the answer or what in the world he was talking about. Then one brave soul spoke up and asked him to clarify. He once again said, "What's in the box?" Met by more confused faces he finally explained, "What is in the box is what Coca-Cola is. The meaning of Coca-Cola and what it means to the consumer." At that point the executives began to see his meaning and discussed the foundational essence of their product. The company had assumed that "great taste" was in the box when in fact what made Coca-Cola successful was "tradition." They, as a company, had failed to keep the main thing the main thing. They had drifted from what made Coke a great product.

What is in your box? What is the foundation of your life? The answer to this is critical because from your box, or main thing, or foundation, flows everything else in your life—including leadership. In order to be a leader you must first build a foundation that can support the life that you will live, the values you will promote, and the principles you will esteem. Your foundation consists of your core assumptions about life, mainly your assumptions about the nature of God and the nature of man.[3] From these assumptions flow your thoughts, attitudes, and actions. These core assumptions have a beginning and that is a relationship. The relationship is either with yourself or with Jesus Christ. If you choose yourself, you will have only yourself to rely upon to accomplish your objective. To be sure, I would not count on myself to lead a dog around the block, much less men and women around this world.

This life you propose to live as a leader is weighty and requires a solid and deep foundation. The heavier the building, the deeper the foundation needs to be. The same is true with people. If a significant foundation is not built before beginning to build upon it, the life above it will risk collapse when the storms of life come—and they *will* come.

The essential element of leadership that is attained through a relationship with Christ is the indwelling of the Holy Spirit. He becomes your compass and guidepost as you navigate through the maze of leading others. Without the strength and assistance of the Holy Spirit in your life, it will be impossible to achieve the character necessary for effective servant leadership. The Holy Spirit is your partner, instructor, and energy source in this venture and will be able to give appropriate guidance regarding tough decisions, ambitious plans, and vital relationships.

When Jesus was training His disciples concerning the Holy Spirit, He said, "But the Counselor, the Holy Spirit, whom the Father will send in my name, will teach you all things…" (John 14:26). Jesus knew of the difficult days that were ahead for the disciples. After Jesus' ascension, they would become the leaders of this mission. They would face far greater burdens than you and I will ever encounter, but with the benefit of the same Helper. The Holy Spirit gave them the tools and knowledge to lead in a Christ-like manner.

What an advantage we have as Christians who take up the banner of leadership! Those that do not know Christ do not have the Holy Spirit for guidance. But those that have the Holy Spirit through a relationship with Jesus Christ have direction. We see this truth in Romans 8:14, "…those who are led by the Spirit of God are sons of God." Those that are not Christians are led by their sin nature, a nature inherent to all men (Romans 5:8). They are slaves to sin (that which offends God) and their life is directed by that nature. God's Word tells us as Christians that we are no longer bound to follow that old nature. It says, "For we know that our old self was crucified with him so that the body of sin might be done away with, that we should no longer be slaves to sin" (Romans 6:6). As a Christian you no longer need to be subject to the old nature but are free to be directed by your new nature given by the Holy Spirit.

Is a relationship with Jesus Christ your foundation? Is He in your box? Is He the main thing in your life? If not, the principles you are about to learn will be an academic exercise and will lead only to frustration in the future, because you will not have the Holy Spirit to make success possible. The archetype of leadership is Jesus Christ, and His Spirit provides strength, wisdom, courage, and supernatural gifting. As Jesus Christ is the Alpha and Omega, He is the beginning and end of leadership. To pursue leadership without a relationship with Christ is like trying to pull a coal train with a tricycle. You look busy but nothing much is really happening. To know more about having this relationship with Jesus Christ, you can look in the appendix in the back of this book. If He is your foundation, then you are ready for the construction crews to move ahead.

Creating you

We do not invent ourselves. As William James put it, "Each of us is in fact what he is almost exclusively by virtue of his imitativeness."[4] We are a patchwork of characteristics of those we have allowed ourselves to be around. We begin with a certain bent that is inherited and not unique by any means. Adam's nature is the beginning of our character and we spend the rest of our lives, as Christians, striving to replace that old nature with that of Christ's. Adam's nature is self-centered, rejects God's standards, and seeks fleshly desires. We cannot overthrow Adam by our own power; instead we must trust Christ to wash away our sin and fill us with His Spirit, freeing us to begin to conform to His image. As we choose His ways over our natural ways, we add to a character that is pleasing to God.

9

Like a chef adding ingredients to a soup, we continually add character traits to our own package. We receive them from others we hang out with, from those we admire, and from those who have authority over us. This imitation begins with our parents and continues through our life. Innocently, we pick up accents, walks, and other mannerisms—but more significantly, we acquire attitudes, character qualities, and destinies.

Kanakuk Kamp is the largest Christian sports camp in America, with ten locations and 10,000 campers each summer. During my college days, I served as a staff member there in Branson, Missouri. A key part of their camp curriculum was based on who the camper's hero was. We would ask the question in small groups and discuss the importance of choosing your heroes carefully. The principle that was taught is that the character qualities you admire will be those that you adopt. That principle is so true. Just like a master and his dog begin to look like each other, so too the hero and the admirer.

The question that you must constantly answer as you develop as a person is not who you want to be, but rather who you want to be like. The Gonzalez family was one of my favorites when I worked at T Bar M Sports Camp in Texas. I always looked forward to seeing their two boys bound through the gates of camp. I never realized how important the relationships of camp were to them until their mother explained it to me and Johnny Polk, my friend and teammate. She said, "Randy, you better not mess up in your life. Because we have a picture of you and Johnny in the boys' room and when facing difficult decisions we ask them what *you* would do in that circumstance. They want to be just like you." Wow! W.W.R.D.? – What Would Randy Do? This humbled me greatly and also reminded me of the parrot principle. We imitate those we admire. So, be careful who you aspire to be like.

Who do you want to be like? In considering leadership, the foremost example of excellence is undoubtedly Jesus Christ. And to pursue leadership, He must be more than a hero. Think about some typical heroes: Michael Jordan, Amy Grant, David Robinson, Orel Hershiser, George Washington, Reggie White,

Abraham Lincoln, Tiger Woods, Elisabeth Eliot, Billy Graham. Wouldn't it be great to actually know these heroes personally, hang out at their house, go on vacations with them, work with them side by side, and talk with them on the phone? How much would they influence your life if you spent personal time with them? Incredibly, we have that opportunity with Jesus. We can relate to Him as well as admire Him from afar.

Your purpose on earth

If Jesus Christ is more than a hero to you, then you should understand God's purpose for you. God's purpose for man is to become Christ-like. In Romans 8:28 we find the promise that "all things work together for good for those who love the Lord and are called according to His purpose." We all rest in the fact that God has a plan for us that is both bright and beautiful. But most people fail to recognize what that purpose Paul speaks of is. Fortunately, God follows up with that purpose immediately in verse 29: "For those God foreknew he also predestined to be conformed to the likeness of his Son..." God knew us before we were born...He has predetermined a purpose for us...that purpose is to be Christ-like.

So God's purpose for us is to be conformed to who Jesus is, to take on His character and attitudes. In 2 Corinthians 5:20, Paul says we are to be ambassadors for Christ. An ambassador is not only a representative but a near-duplicate of someone else. If you were to be my ambassador to a meeting I couldn't attend, you would first spend time with me, find out what I wanted done at that meeting, how I would act at the meeting, and then take my place there. As an ambassador, you would represent me to the degree that it would be as if I were there. An ambassador does not speak on his own authority nor does he act on his own. He acts and thinks as the one who sent him would. I am sure there are times that every ambassador at the United Nations has considered voting as he sees fit instead of on behalf of his country. But to do so

11

would make him a sovereign agent and no longer an ambassador. You can see now how our ambassadorship for Christ radically changes the way we look at life and more specifically leadership.

This purpose shouldn't come as a revelation to the Christian, but surprisingly, non-Christians expect this Christ-likeness as well.

As a director of T Bar M Sports Camp, I had the opportunity to see Christ-likeness in action on a daily basis. The college staff that worked as counselors during the summer season represented Christ in many ways. The directors expected this of themselves and of the staff. What I became aware of one summer was that the campers expected Christ-likeness as well. One situation drove this point home for me in a dramatic way. During one camp session a camper and counselor had a disagreement that quickly became a deadlock of wills. The counselor had made some unreasonable request of the camper (something like, "You can't swim the rest of your time at camp"), and the camper had overreacted in an aggressive manner. I was called in to sort out the situation. I met with the counselor to get his side of the story and then with the camper to hear his. The camper was about nine years old but mature for his age. He was also Jewish, which was unusual because the camp was overtly Christian. He told me about what had happened and apologized for his behavior. Then, through tears and with a quiver in his voice, he said something that I won't soon forget. Commenting on what he observed in the counselor's behavior he said, "Christians aren't supposed to act like that." I was floored because he was right. Here was someone outside the Christian faith who expected Christians to have a higher standard of conduct: an expectation of Christ-likeness.

Christ-likeness demands excellence

During medieval times all skilled laborers were required to endure strenuous training to achieve competence in their craft. To be excellent meant years of work under those who were excellent themselves. Workers progressed from intern to apprentice to journeyman, and then, if they were skilled enough, they became a master craftsman.

These masters formed guilds or unions that protected their vocation from shoddy work that would damage the reputation of the profession. To be a member of a particular guild meant that you had progressed through the plenary levels and achieved a level of excellence in that skill.

One of these guilds was comprised of carpenters who were well known for their abilities in woodworking and most renowned for their skill in making doors. If anyone at that time was building a beautiful home or magnificent cathedral, they would call upon this guild to build the portals. The members of this guild were also Christians. They wanted to make sure that whoever saw their doors would know that the excellence displayed by their work was because of Jesus Christ. So with this in mind, they designed a door that was their hallmark (figure 3). You have probably seen it before in buildings and homes of today. Most likely you have one in

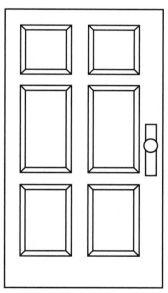

figure 3

your own home. As you look at it, you see a cross in the upper two-thirds of the door and an open Bible in the lower portion. The excellence of these committed Christians still influences us centuries later. This should be the goal for every Christian: does the world see the excellence of your life and attribute that to your relationship with Christ?

With the world's expectation, our own expectation, and God's expectation that we represent Christ well, it is not hard to see the consequences of not becoming Christ-like while claiming the faith. I have a friend who was involved in campus ministry at Rice University in Houston. Rice is one of the most academically challenging and respected schools in the nation. During a discussion we were having about the ineffectiveness of ministries on the Rice campus, he made an interesting statement. He said, "The reason the Gospel has not had a greater impact on the campus is because Christians at Rice are such poor students." This observation by my friend was a great example of the world's expectation of excellence in the lives of Christians. The gospel didn't seem compelling without a physical example to validate it.

Christians have an obligation to be Christ-like by example whether it is in conduct, speech, or attitude. As this is manifested in day-to-day excellence, Christians will have the opportunity to point to the source of their excellence, Jesus Christ.

Successful leadership

How will you know when you are a successful leader? You are successful as a leader when you reach your goal of being Christ-like. You fail when you do not. It is a cycle that begins with Christ-likeness and ends with the same.

Wes Neal, the author of several books on Christ-likeness, taught me a lot about winning and success. Early in my career I spent a year training with Wes. One of many lessons I learned from him was that winning in God's eyes does not have anything to do with the scoreboard, grades, accomplishments, money, fame, or awards. Winning is, by definition, reaching a predetermined goal. And for the Christian that goal is Christ-likeness.

An example of winning on the scoreboard while losing in life is that of coach Jimmy Johnson. A few years ago, when Johnson was head coach of the Dallas Cowboys, he was asked about balancing his personal and family life with that of his profession. Johnson explained that for him and his team to be successful, he must sacrifice time with his family. Practically, this meant completely turning his back on his wife and children. In an interview with the *Dallas Morning News,* Johnson reflected on the differences between coaching at the college level and coaching in the pros. He said, "There are a lot of social functions to deal with in being a college football coach, and I don't have them any more. In my opinion, it was good I was married there. It would have been a little more of a negative getting a divorce in college. Here, not a lot of explanations had to be made."[5] He went on to win two Super Bowls with the Cowboys and was hailed as a great coach. No doubt this philosophy of life is one familiar to most in our culture. Since winning is the only thing in our world, it stands to reason that everything you have is worth sacrificing for that purpose.

Men and women who are called "leaders" in our culture and give away all to attain greatness are admired, esteemed, and usually well-paid. But what is more difficult? Sacrificing your family, vital relationships, service, or other satellite associations— or sacrificing yourself? There is no honor in the former and certainly no virtue. Only by sacrificing yourself will true leadership be attainable. And the essence of this sacrifice is found in Philippians 2:3-5: "Do nothing out of selfish ambition or vain conceit, but in humility consider others better than yourselves. Each of you should look not only to your own interests, but also to the interests of others. Your attitude should be the same as that of Christ Jesus."

What you know now...
- What or who is the main thing in your life?
- You become like who you admire.
- Christ-likeness is God's purpose for you.
- Christ-likeness is the foundation of leadership.
- Success as a servant leader is Christ-likeness, and Christ-likeness is success.

CHAPTER ONE
Study Section

Have you ever stood beneath an oak tree? It is an awe-inspiring experience. When you stand next to a full-grown oak, its massiveness is almost overwhelming. The sheer width of the tree's trunk and its mighty stature quickly remind you of how small you are and how big God is.

What is even more fascinating about these mighty oaks is their incredible strength against adverse weather conditions. An oak can often withstand the fiercest of storms and come out with relatively little damage. And uproot a full-grown oak tree? Nearly impossible! You see the strongest part of the oak tree is hidden beneath the ground. An oak tree's roots grow as long as it is high, stretching themselves out in every direction. And these are no pushover roots. They are strong and tough, firmly planted and unwilling to move. When the roots of an oak tree establish a foundation in an area that is conducive to their growth, they become unwavering, and that is why the oak is one of the strongest trees in the world.

As Christians it is important that we too are firmly rooted, like the oak, so that when the storms of life come rolling our way, we can withstand them. Before we can stretch out our roots, however, we need to plant ourselves upon a solid foundation—one that is strong and immovable by outside forces. Let's begin by turning to the Word and testing our foundation.

A Message from the Word

"By the grace God has given me, I laid a foundation as an expert builder, and someone else is building on it. But each one should be careful how he builds. For no one can lay any foundation other than the one already laid, which is Jesus Christ. If any man builds on this foundation using gold, silver, costly stones, wood, hay or straw, his work will be shown for what it is, because the Day will bring it to light. It will be revealed with fire and the fire will test the quality of each man's work. If what he built survives, he will receive his reward. If it is destroyed, he will suffer loss. He himself will be saved, but only as one escaping through the flames."

1 Corinthians 3:10-15

In his book, "Just Like Jesus," Max Lucado describes Christ in the following passage:

"The world has never known a heart so pure, a character so flawless. His spiritual hearing was so keen he never missed a heavenly whisper. His mercy so abundant he never missed a chance to forgive. No lie left his lips, no distraction marred his vision. He touched when others recoiled. He endured when others quit. Jesus is the model for every person...[God] urges you to fix your eyes upon Jesus. Heaven invites you to set the lens of your heart on the Savior and make him the object of your life."[6]

When Paul wrote to the Corinthians, he wanted them to understand the importance of Christ being the foundation upon which they should build. You see, Christ has already laid the foundation for us; all we have to do is build upon it using materials that will withstand the test of fire. But how do we do this? What are the precious jewels that we must use in order to "lay a foundation as an expert builder" as Paul did?

Let's go back to the oak tree for a moment. If the tree is planted in an area where there is little sunlight and water, the root system will be weak and frail. In fact, when a tree is lacking water, often its roots will begin to grow up towards the surface of the ground in the hopes of receiving some nourishment. But when the roots of a tree are exposed, nothing can protect it from the gusts of wind that roll by, and it will not survive.

Each day, you will experience new trials and hardships. As you trod through life, you learn lessons from these trials. The application of these lessons into your life brings about wisdom. They establish your roots in Christ's nourishing soil. These life lessons are some of the precious jewels that you can use to build upon your foundation of Christ.

Other materials that are "fireproof" are the characteristics of Christ that you will inevitably adopt as you further study His Word and spend time in His presence. These actions water your soul allowing you to flourish under Christ's control. You must understand that these things are key if you are going to be a Christ-like example. Even Jesus understood the importance of prayer, scripture memory and Bible study. These are the building blocks to the Christ-like attitude of a godly leader.

Without the Word, you are like an oak tree without roots. There is no nourishment, no support system and no strength. One gust of wind, and you come crashing to the ground—you don't stand a chance.

Christ is the foundation, and His characteristics are the materials needed to successfully mold you into a leader who brings glory to His Name.

Reflection

Make a list of the people and things that are most important to you. Why?

my parents - loving, caring and I respect them so much for their hard work and intelligence.

Are you looking for nourishment in areas other than Christ Himself? _parents!_

Is Christ the center of everything you do? Why or why not?

No. Many times I am selfish and I try doing things for myself and not Christ.

Years ago, Gatorade ran a campaign slogan with Michael Jordan as their spokesman. "I want to be like Mike," reverberated through households all over America as pictures of the basketball legend floated across our TV screens.

Who do you want to be like? If you had to replace Michael Jordan's name with someone else's, who would you insert?

I don't think there is anyone I would want to be. Sometimes there are people who I'd want to look like though.

What character qualities would you like to develop in your own life?

I'd want to be more voiced, forgiving, accepting, thankful, and able to minister to others.

Take a few moments to think about some things that you need to change in order to build a stronger foundation. What are some areas in your life that need strengthening as you begin your quest for leadership? List any thoughts that come to your mind in the space provided below. Ask the Lord to reveal to you any areas that you may not be able to see.

One thing I need to change is focusing on God as opposed to only school or only homework, or procrastinating to later Stress myself out. I need to get up and find a church that actually speaks to me. I need to witness to more people but I lack the reaching voice.

What is Leadership?

J. Oswald Sanders defines "leadership" in his classic work on the subject as "influence, the ability of one person to influence others."[1] In an Army pamphlet entitled Leadership at Senior Levels of Command, the term is further clarified: "Leadership is defined as the process of influencing the actions of individuals and organizations in order to obtain desired results."[2]

If you were to list the greatest leaders of all time you would no doubt include George Washington, David, Moses, Booker T. Washington, Joan of Arc, Martin Luther King, Winston Churchill, and the Apostle Paul, but according to these definitions you would also have to include Alexander the Great, Joseph Stalin, Adolph Hitler, and Mao Tse Tung. How can Moses and Hitler both be great leaders?

All of these were great leaders because they had great influence. Obviously they each had different styles, goals, and values—but they, nonetheless, had one thing in common and that was "influence." They were able to mobilize people toward a goal beyond themselves, whether good or evil, and motivate those followers to action. Influence is not difficult. We influence those around us all the time. We do this without even thinking about it. The trick is to influence for good rather than evil.

You influence and are influenced on a daily basis—actually moment by moment. So it is important that you understand how easy it is to influence and be influenced.

Let's take a little math test. As you look at the addition problem below, what would you say is the answer?

$$
\begin{array}{r}
1000 \\
40 \\
1000 \\
30 \\
1000 \\
20 \\
1000 \\
+\ \ 10 \\
\hline
5000
\end{array}
$$

You probably answered 5000, right? Wrong! Take another look and you will see that the answer is actually 4100! Why did you answer a simple addition problem incorrectly? Most likely because I showed you the wrong answer—I influenced you. I led you to the answer I wanted you to give.

Consider the influence others have on you. Do you act differently depending on who you are around? We all do. As the Director for Worldview Academy Leadership Camps, I travel all around the country. Regional accents, customs, and attitudes that differ from my Texas heritage are distinct and diverse. When I'm in the Midwest, I'll begin saying "you guys," in the South "y'all," and in the Northwest "yooz guys." Each region influences my perfect Texas drawl. After returning home, it may take days to return to a proper dialect.

You may influence others in more ways than you know. I've heard the story of a young girl who was placed in a mental institution. To see her at first glance, one would think nothing wrong. But she was completely closed to the outside world and spent most of her days curled into a fetal position unwilling to communicate with anyone. Her parents tried everything to bring her back to life but finally were left with no choice but to have her committed. She was placed in a padded chamber that was more of a prison cell than a hospital room. Each day she could be observed rolled into a ball in the corner of her cell—no communication, no touch, no laughter, no love, no childhood. She was given three meals a day on a tray slid under a gap below the heavy steel door, but she usually ignored the food.

Each night, when most of the institution's staff had gone home, an old cleaning woman would dutifully sweep the long hallways. As she tended to her chores, she would pause at each cell door and, on her tiptoes, peek in on the "prisoners" through the grated door window. From the first day of the young girl's internment, this old woman took a special interest in her. She would notice that her dinner tray had not been touched and so she would crouch down on one knee, take her broom handle and push the tray over to the little cocoon. Then she would tap her on the knee and softly say, "Somebody loves you, honey. Somebody cares." She would slowly rise and continue her cleaning duties. Each night the same scene could be witnessed. A kneel, a push, a tap, and the words, "Somebody loves you, honey. Somebody cares."

As the days turned to weeks, and weeks to months, the young bud began to open. To the surprise of the doctors, the little girl started to communicate—slowly at first and then with purpose. It was as though she was raised from the dead. She was later released and went to school. She excelled and as she grew up, found an interest and aptitude in teaching. She became a teacher and committed herself to help others who were stricken with similar conditions that she had battled. She eventually encountered a student who was as much of a challenge as she must have been. The student's name: Helen Keller. The teacher, the young girl who had been left for dead, and only touched by a caring old cleaning woman in a mental institution, was Ann Sullivan.

This elderly chambermaid is nameless and faceless, but she had an influence on the world that lasts to this day. Your influence most times will be as anonymous, but likely no less powerful in its own way.

With influence being as natural in our daily lives as breathing and eating, you can imagine the importance of influencing or leading from a Christ-like perspective.

Leadership is influence; influence is power

When you are a leader, you will have power. The man or woman who can influence others to behave in ways they wouldn't ordinarily choose exerts real control and real power. Christians, of course, recognize that such power should be used responsibly. We will discuss in detail later on just what you are to do with that power. But remember that to lead is a risky business—you will have an extra share of temptations. For as T.B. Macaulay once wrote, "The highest proof of virtue is to possess boundless power without abusing it."[3]

The Sacred / Secular Trap

Take a sheet of paper and draw a line down the middle from top to bottom. On each side of that line write the words "spiritual" and "secular" like you see below (Figure 4). In the spiritual column, list those spiritual things you do on a weekly basis. Now under the secular column, list the secular things you do during the week.

Spiritual	Secular
pray. go to church. worshipping. reading the bible.	homework. shopping. ice-skating movies. tennis.

figure 4

Most likely on the spiritual side of your life you listed prayer, church, Bible study, fellowship, witnessing, worship. Under the secular part of your life you put music, TV, computer, school, work, movies, shopping, politics, sports, etc. You probably placed everything other than the six "spiritual" items under the secular. But such a list is unbiblical!

This view of life is unbiblical in that it assumes that God is not concerned about those *other* areas of our life that do not have the outward appearances of spirituality. Christians must remember that God is concerned about those areas and every other area of our daily living. The Psalmist confirmed this in saying "The earth is the LORD's, and everything in it" (Psalms 24:1). Every choice, every action, every attitude is either pleasing or displeasing to God, no matter how insignificant it may seem to us. C.S. Lewis once wrote, "There is no neutral ground in the universe. Every square inch, every split second is claimed by God and counter-claimed by Satan."[4] The snare that most of us fall into is the belief that everything that we do is either spiritual (sacred) or worldly (secular). We have bought into the idea that life is compartmentalized into sections that are separate and unassociated. For example, many Americans agree with President Bill Clinton's assertion that his private life and public life are unrelated.

The truth of the matter is that nothing man influences remains neutral. Once a person steps into leadership, he or she becomes either pleasing or displeasing to God. Again, Sanders says it well: "Since leadership is essentially the power of one man to influence another, it is well to consider the almost limitless possibilities of a single life for good or ill. Both Scripture and experience affirm that no one can be neutral, either morally or spiritually. On lives that come within the range of our influence we leave an indelible impression, whether we are conscious of it or not. Dr. John Geddie, for example, went to Aneityum in 1848 and worked there for God for twenty-four years. On the tablet erected to his memory these words are inscribed:

When he landed, in 1848, there were no Christians.
When he left, in 1872, there were no heathen."[5]

Lead, don't push

To influence is to lead. This is different than to push. One of the first skills we learn as children is not to push other children, whether we are in line or on the playground. That lesson is a good one that holds true in leadership. An old Texas cowboy adage says, "It's easier to lead a mule than to push him—especially if the mule has had a bad day." People are the same way, and so the gentle leader is less likely to be kicked.

Leadership guru Ken Blanchard describes it this way: "The key to successful leadership today is influence, not authority."[6] If leadership is influence then it is not leverage, coercion, or manipulation. It is not a whip or a carrot on a stick. By leading we influence, not by deception or insincerity, but by truth and forthrightness. A leader must understand that those he leads desire to excel but will not unless encouraged, challenged and rewarded. I once heard former Dallas Cowboys head coach Tom Landry say that "the job of a coach is to make the players do what they would not do on their own to become the players they want to be." As Ralph Waldo Emerson said, "Our chief want in life is somebody who shall make us do what we can."[7]

The world pushes, a servant leads. In teaching His disciples principles in leadership, Jesus said, "You know that those who are recognized as rulers of the Gentiles lord it over them; and their great men exercise authority over them. But it is not this way among you, but whoever wishes to become great among you shall be your servant; and whoever wishes to be first among you shall be slave of all" (Mark 10:42-43). A leader doesn't lord, exercise authority, give guilt trips, manipulate, or push. As a leader you are a servant who assists others in becoming the person they desire to be, reaching the goals to which they aspire. Booker T. Washington said it well: "There are two ways of exerting one's strength: one is pushing down, the other is pulling up."[8]

The Sphere

*"A man who wants to lead the orchestra must turn
his back on the crowd."–Anonymous*

Surrounding each one of us is a sphere of influence (see Figure 5) that can be our greatest resource or our worst enemy. This sphere is the "affect field" around an individual which includes relationships, institutions, environment, and resources.

There are six of us in the Sims family. At any time, any one of us affects all of us (or is it infects!). When we get in the car for a trip, this principle is magnified. As is the case in most family cars, each child passenger creates a sovereign territory around himself. Imaginary border lines are drawn, implied treaties are agreed to, and each rider protects his "turf" and airspace. In the midst of van world peace, Stacy, age 9, violates Bryan's, age 12, space by putting her foot on "his side" of the seat. Bryan, detecting the invasion on his radar, throws a pillow at Stacy to remind her of his territory, but it misses her and hits Travis, age 6, who then

figure 5

instinctively swings a book in retaliation, hitting Gracie, age 2, in the head. Gracie lets out a scream (her only weapon against foreign threats) that cracks the windshield. At this point, Mom, age unknown, reaches for the "spank stick" which is a Wal-Mart paint stirring stick. As with most mothers, she is a master at using this instrument. No Jedi Knight, armed only with a light saber, would dare tangle with a mother wielding a spank stick. A barrage of "he did it"—"she did it" comes back toward the front seat when I, with fatherly wisdom, of course, threaten to pull the van over and spank everyone by the side of the interstate. Did each one of us have power through influence? Absolutely! Each of us influenced the sphere around us and was influenced by that same sphere.

30

Who's influencing who?

The sphere will be influenced by the leader and influence the leader.

As a leader, you must be discerning in filtering that influence and exerting your own influence. What influences will you allow to affect you, and what will be the influences you intend? Daniel was a young leader who found himself in grave circumstances. He and his people were exiled to Babylon and forced to learn the customs and language of a wicked culture. He could have been assimilated completely by the influence of that new culture—worshipping idols and ignoring God—but Daniel committed to rejecting ungodly influences and only accepting those that were pleasing to his God. He then began to influence the sphere around him with an example of excellence and integrity.

Each time Daniel was faithful to God's standard his sphere became larger, until finally he was in line to lead the entire kingdom. After Darius, came to power we learn of the extent of Daniel's influence: "Now Daniel so distinguished himself among the administrators [leaders] and the satraps by his exceptional qualities that the king planned to set him over the whole kingdom" (Daniel 6:3). It is amazing that a prisoner/slave could rise to such a level of influence. But by staying true to God, he was given an increasingly larger sphere of influence.

As leaders, we take on the responsibility of our influence; to be a servant leader, we must lead with a Christ-like example. Albert Schweitzer said, "Example is not the main thing in influencing others. It is the only thing."[9]

Jesus also had a sphere of influence around Him. The sphere consisted of His disciples, occasional followers and listeners, and the Pharisees. He was tempted continually by His sphere to compromise His mission—especially by the Pharisees. They came to Jesus on one occasion and asked Him one of their trick questions in an effort to trap Him. But before they asked the question, they made a statement that was true of Jesus and His ability to influence and not be influenced by the sphere. The Pharisees approached Jesus and said, "Teacher...we know you are a man of integrity and that you teach the way of God in accordance with the truth. You aren't swayed by men, because you pay no attention to who they are" (Matthew 22:16). Even the Pharisees recognized how Jesus conducted Himself as a leader who was not influenced by the wrong elements in His sphere.

King Saul wielded great influence and was therefore a great leader, but he also allowed the sphere to dictate his decisions in a negative way. In 1 Samuel 15, the Bible tells us about King Saul's conquest of the Amalekites. He was commanded to utterly destroy the Amalekite—everyone and everything, including livestock. He did destroy the Amalekites but kept the choice livestock at the urging of his men. When confronted by the Lord through Samuel, he first lied and then blamed his people. This strategy of escaping responsibility may sound familiar. Saul's eventual answer to Samuel's direct question is found in 1 Samuel 15:24: "[I did it] *because I feared the people and listened to their voice*" [italics added].

Saul sought the approval of his followers rather than the approval of the Lord, and so his kingdom was removed from him and he was rejected as a leader. In a prophecy pointing to David's future leadership and the rejection of Saul's leadership, 1 Samuel 13:14 states: "But now your kingdom will not endure; the LORD has sought out a man after his own heart and appointed him leader of his people, because you have not kept the LORD's command." You will have many opportunities to choose God over men, and vice versa. How you decide can make or break you as a leader—as it did Saul.

The thermostat principle

Another way to look at our sphere of influence is to imagine ourselves as either a thermostat or a thermometer. The servant leader influences his sphere as a thermostat affects the environment of a house. The thermostat in a building sets the temperature and monitors its changes. Consider the life of Bishop Evin Berggrav, a leader in the Norwegian Lutheran Church during World War II. He was unjustly imprisoned for his beliefs and teachings in defiance of the Nazis. During his imprisonment, he received unusual treatment from his captors: the 12-man guard was changed every two hours to minimize the spiritual influence he would have on them! Clearly, Berggrav dictated the spiritual and emotional climate around him.

Unfortunately, most times we allow ourselves to be more like a thermometer. We fluctuate according to the surroundings, environment, and circumstances. A thermometer leader is not stable. His temperature rises when the environment is hot and plummets when it is cold. As a leader, you must maintain a constant temperature. Those around you will depend upon your consistent ability to remain focused on the goal even when the circumstances are fluctuating.

The hard work of leadership

"In business or in football, it takes a lot of unspectacular preparation to produce spectacular results."
– Roger Staubach[10]

Let's not get too romantic about leadership—it is hard work. Leadership is not necessarily stretch limos, corner offices, big houses, fame, and a bio in People magazine. Edmund Burke once said that "The only training for the heroic is the mundane."[11] In preparing for leadership you must do the unseen, unappreciated, and unsung labor of developing yourself. The ordinary, day-to-day tasks that we all do (taking out the trash, making the bed, doing homework, yardwork, setting up chairs at church, etc.) are forging in us valuable virtues. Developing these elements of your skillset most likely will go unnoticed. At the outset only you will be aware of the growth, but the change will be noticed by others as your willingness to serve is put into practice. As Blaise Pascal wrote, "The extent of a man's virtue ought not be measured by his [special] efforts, but by his usual behavior."[12]

"Little" work pays off big

We so often downplay the importance of the "little" things in our life—but it is the mundane and the ordinary that challenge us the most. Anyone can work hard when they're thrust on stage; the trick is to work hard when no one seems to be watching. The San Francisco 49er's Jerry Rice is arguably the greatest receiver in the history of the NFL. He is the greatest on gameday *because* he is the greatest on Monday through Saturday. According to his coaches and teammates, he is the first one on the practice field and the last one to leave. Rice is so committed to the minutia of his craft that he creates drills for himself that hone the smallest detail of catching passes. Only his team sees all this extra effort, but every fan sees and appreciates the results on Sunday. It takes a lot of effort to make something difficult appear effortless.

Oh, how the little things turn into big things. Several years ago a man walked from San Francisco to New York. It took several years to complete the journey. When he had finished, the media clamored for interviews. One interviewer asked him what was the greatest challenge he had faced in his continental traverse. The reporter expected the Rocky Mountains, desert heat, or perhaps the loneliness of vast prairies to be the biggest obstacle. But the sojourner answered, "It was the sand in my shoes." Grains of sand! The greatest challenge was not mountains, storms, nor distance but the little things.

A hairline fracture in a dam.

An undetected flaw in a heart pacemaker.

An unprepared soldier on the battle line.

A weak spot in a gondola cable.

A small tear in a rappelling rope.

An exposed electrical wire in a house.

A pinhole leak in an automobile brake line.

When the small is ignored, prepare to deal with disaster.

Get up and go to work

"There is no substitute for hard work."
– Thomas A. Edison[13]

Yes, preparing for leadership is hard work. Now is the time to get off the couch, bequeath the TV remote to your little brother, and get busy. It's no wonder that there is a book in the Bible called the *Acts of the Apostles* and not the *Good Intentions of the Apostles or the Plans of the Apostles*. Those men of God did something with what they were given.

If three frogs are sitting on a log and two of them decide to jump in the pond, how many frogs are left on the log? Three. Deciding to do something and doing it are different altogether. You've decided you want to be a leader—now jump. Know that the principle of reaping and sowing found in Galations 6 is dependent upon sowing. With your sowing, you will see the results. So many Christians give up on leadership before they get started because they see the hard work that is before them. G.K. Chesterton's wise words remind us of this principle: "The Christian ideal has not been tried and found wanting. It has been found difficult; and left untried."[14]

What you know now...
- Leadership is influence.
- Dividing life into sacred and secular compartments is an unbiblical view of reality.
- Each of us has a sphere of influence that we affect and by which we are affected.
- Leadership is hard work.
- Take the initiative to do that hard work.

C H A P T E R   T W O
Study Section

Grand Ole Opry star Jerry Clower is best known for his comic stories of growing up in Yazoo City, Mississippi, with friends like Marcel and Clovis Ledbetter. Clower entertained thousands of people with his hilarious antics of coon hunting in the Deep South.

Jerry Clower grew up dirt poor in the cotton fields of Mississippi. His one ambition in life was to become a 4-H County agent, so he set out to accomplish that goal. After he did that, Clower began selling fertilizer as a means to get by. Since he didn't have a hugely exciting job, he tried to make things more interesting by telling stories. When someone overheard him storytelling, Jerry became an almost overnight success. Soon MCA records offered him a record deal, and the "Loudmouthest" Daddy from Yazoo City became a national star.

In the summer of 1991, JoAnn Prichard of the University Press of Mississippi caught up with Jerry at his Mississippi home. The interview was later integrated into his book, *Stories from Home*.

One of the questions Prichard asked the comedian was who had an important influence on his life. Jerry responded by describing his old friend and mentor, Owen Cooper. Mr. Cooper had a huge impact on Clower's life, counseling him and encouraging him spiritually and in business. Here is what Jerry Clower said about the man that so profoundly influenced his life:

"If the Lord gave me the ingredients and told me to make a man, I'd make him exactly like Owen Cooper. I knew [Owen] through his pocketbook, I knew him through his family, and I knew him through his business dealings. I've been under fire with him in business. I've been with him in good times. And I've seen him react every time like you're supposed to if you claim to be a maximum, Bible-believing

Southern Baptist Christian. And he never varied in dealing decently and in order with everybody. He was a remarkable, unbelievable person. And brilliant."

Even after his death, Owen Cooper continued to influence Jerry's life. "I [want] his counsel. I miss him," Jerry said. "But I still feel his arms around me every day. When I'm making decisions about my family and about my show business career, I remember the things he taught me."[15]

It was Owen Cooper, and others like him, who believed in the man with the big laugh and even bigger mouth. Because of their encouragement, Jerry Clower had a huge impact on culture. The impact you have on a person could potentially affect him for the rest of his life.

A Message from the Word

"Mordecai left the king's presence wearing royal garments of blue and white, a large crown of gold and a purple robe of fine linen. And the city of Susa held a joyous celebration. For the Jews it was a time of happiness and joy, gladness and honor. Mordecai was prominent in the palace; his reputation spread throughout the provinces, and he became more and more powerful. Mordecai the Jew was second in rank to King Xerxes, preeminent among the Jews, and held in high esteem by his many fellow Jews, because he worked for the good of his people and spoke up for the welfare of all the Jews."

Esther 8:15-17; 9:4; 10:3

When Mordecai learned of King Xerxes' edict to annihilate the Jews, he was not in a position of influence to stop the coming siege. Instead of despairing, however, Mordecai took immediate action. We can learn a lot from the steps that this brave man took in a time of crisis.

First, he cried out to God for mercy and help. With complete faith and trust, Mordecai tore his robes, put on sackcloth and called out to his God.

Second, Mordecai summoned his cousin Esther, who was also Xerxes' wife, and informed her of the plan. Mordecai himself had no way of stopping the issued edict, so he turned to someone who could possibly give him some help.

Mordecai's third influential decision was to encourage Esther to approach her husband. Despite the fact that she was Queen, Esther was in a very precarious position. In those days, the Queen had very few rights and little influence over the affairs of state. It was illegal for Esther to even approach her husband, the king or to summon him, and to break that law was punishable by death.

Before she attempted to appeal to her husband, Esther asked Mordecai to gather all the Jews in Susa and spend three days fasting and praying for her. She would not attempt to contact her husband without God's blessing. Mordecai listened to his cousin's request and faithfully carried out all of her instructions.

Neither Mordecai nor Esther was in a "position" to be great leaders when the king declared his edict. Although having no real position, they exhibited influence in their circumstance. When they realized what needed to be done, they did not lament over their lack of position but instead acted even though they both could have been executed for their actions.

Because of the steps they took, Mordecai and Esther were able to reveal to Xerxes that his assistant had tricked him, and he withdrew his edict against the Jews. Their upright behavior and fair dealings influenced the king mightily, and after that, they both held a position of esteem. Mordecai was even made second in command to the king! The book of Esther ends with a comment on Mordecai's incredible leadership skills. For the rest of his days, Mordecai was in a position of influence, working in close proximity with the king.

Reflection

Is it difficult for you to see yourself as a leader? Why or why not?

Yes. Because I am one of those people who is not comfortable (mostly) in reaching out to others.

While we have the incredible potential to influence others, we are also affected by the influence of those around us. How easily are you influenced?

How has that influence affected you?

Sometimes my actions or manner are influenced by what my family or people at school tell me. But I am content about myself and who and how God has made me.

How do you think you influence others?

I tend to have a really positive attitude that many times will rub off onto others.

Do you think that others respect you? Why or why not?

Yes. because I give my respect to other people and treat everyone the same.

Make a list of the influences in your life, both positive and negative. Put the influences that bring you closer to Christ-likeness (positive) in the left column, and the influences that move you away from Christ-likeness (negative) in the right.

Positive	Negative
Parents	television
Church	movies
youth group.	music
School	School.

What are some things you can do to increase the left column and decrease the right?

Get more involved in Church. Focus on God.

During World War II, when the Germans invaded the Soviet town of Kiev, they took a young girl named Maria captive and sent her to Germany to work in an underground slave labor camp. At fourteen, Maria was the oldest of the children forced to assemble artillery in the death camp. Despite their meager situation, Maria determined to survive. She encouraged the other children imprisoned with her to do the same and she worked hard to keep their spirits up.

When the German soldiers cut back on meals, feeding their

laborers once a day instead of twice, many of the children became very ill. To make matters worse, the food was often infested with maggots and other bugs. Finally, as death began to take over the vulnerable group, Maria stood up to the German guards and demanded better treatment. In response, they beat her viciously.

When a young German nurse heard what happened to Maria, she was furious and rushed to the wounded girl's aid. Although she could have been seriously punished, this young nurse stayed by Maria's side, tending to her until she healed. When Maria was able to talk again, she begged the nurse to look after the younger children. Moved with compassion, the nurse complied with Maria's request. Every day, when the nurse came to visit her patient, Maria asked her how the children were doing. When Maria was strong enough to go back to work, she found that the food was much better and they were once again being fed twice a day.

After two years of living and working underground, the Nazis finally released their prisoners. Out of the 200 children held captive in Maria's camp, 182 of them walked out, alive and fairly well. Their lives were forever indebted to two young women who stood strong in the face of opposition.

When Maria stood up to the guards, she dramatically influenced the outcome of that one slave labor camp. Had she not had the courage to challenge her oppressors, many more children would have died.

Do you know people who need someone to stand up for them? Are you impacting others by strengthening them, or are you allowing them to be beaten by the enemy? Look closely at the people around you. Who needs your encouragement and influence today?

my friend, Ethan, what is right and do not fear.
my parents - do not stress.

Who are the people in your life that you believe you can influence? How can you have a positive effect on their lives?

I believe that I can influence would be my siblings, (they are younger than me so I am their big example.) To have a positive effect on their lives I should act in a Christ-like attitude, be positive, be thankful and a friend so that they may see a "more appropriate" manner to act in. I could also influence my peers. If I stood up and witnessed to my non-believing friends and act in a way to glorify Christ they may pick-up some of those positive Christ-like attributes.

The
Leader
You Will
Be

The leader you will become is not what you are now. You are not the person today you will be tomorrow. The way things are now, you probably don't think of yourself as the next leader of the free world. Your mother may think so, but in reality you're right—you aren't that impressive and neither am I. Now for the good news: potential is not determined by what is seen now but by what is realized in the future.

In his book, *Developing the Leader Within You*, John Maxwell reminds us that greatness often flows out of humble beginnings:

> "Many great people [had humble beginnings].
> Thomas Edison was a newsboy on trains. Andrew
> Carnegie started work at $4 a month, John D.

Rockefeller at $6 a week. The remarkable thing about Abraham Lincoln was not that he was born in a log cabin, but that he got out of the log cabin. Demosthenes, the greatest orator of the ancient world, stuttered! The first time he tried to make a public speech, he was laughed off the rostrum. Julius Caesar was an epileptic. Napoleon was of humble parentage and far from being a born genius (he stood forty-sixth in his class at the Military Academy in a class of sixty-five). Beethoven was deaf, as was Thomas Edison. Charles Dickens was lame; so was Handel. Homer was blind; Plato was a hunchback; Sir Walter Scott was paralyzed."[1]

These future leaders had much to overcome—probably more than you. But they saw past the present and toward what they could be. Who you are now is not who you will become. So begin to see yourself as you can be—not what you are.

The story is told of a professor who walked into his class each day, doffed his hat, and bowed with graceful honor before his students. When asked by someone why he did this, he responded, "Because I believe one day a leader will emerge from these young men and I desire to honor him." Years later one of his young students, Martin Luther, distinguished himself by leading the Reformation. I am sure that as Martin Luther sat there as a pupil, he did not appear to be a world-changer, but his mentor saw past appearances and had faith in who someone in his class could become. Do you see yourself as having potential for greatness?

The image in the mirror is not you

Each morning, when you look in the bathroom mirror to see if there were any improvements overnight, you see someone you know all too well. That person is one who is developing but not yet complete. Tomorrow morning take a closer look (be careful not to put a nose print on the mirror) and see the someone who isn't reflected there. That person is who you will become.

We may choose to see ourselves as we are, as others see us, or to look beyond. The story is told of a kid named Jimmy. He was just a young boy when his father passed away and, as the oldest of several children, he had to find work to help support the family. Jimmy was hired by a kindly farmer named Johnson and began working after school and during the summers. Jimmy faithfully planted, tilled, and harvested for several years. As Jimmy worked on the farm, he and the farmer's beautiful daughter, Sally, built up a friendship that soon grew into fondness. As was the custom of the day, Jimmy went to Old Man Johnson and asked if it would be okay if he courted Sally.

Old Man Johnson thought for a brief moment as he rubbed his sun-leathered brow. Then he looked down into Jimmy's hopeful eyes. "You know, Jimmy, I think you're a fine young man and you do everything I ask you to do around the farm." Old Man Johnson paused to find the right words for what he wanted to say. "Jimmy, I'm wanting something special for my little Sally; I'm wanting someone that is going to take her off of this old farm and take care of her like I've never been able to. Someone who has ambition. A man with potential." The crusty old farmer's eyes grew softer trying to ease the blow of what he was about to say. "But Jimmy, I don't think you're the boy to do that for Sally. In fact I think it would be a good idea if you and Sally didn't socialize anymore."

Jimmy's heart sank. He was crushed. Jimmy was so hurt that he left the farm that day and left the small town. He ran off, lied about his age, and joined the army. The years went by, Old Man Johnson passed away, and Sally grew up and met the man that took her off the farm. She moved to the city and had children who had children of their own.

One day Sally gathered the whole family together, and they took a trip to the old homestead where she had grown up. As they arrived, Sally went to the front door of her old house, now belonging to someone else, to ask permission to tour the farm with her family. The owners gladly granted it, and Sally began to relate to her "city slicker" family what it was like to grow up on a farm.

In the barn, Sally was explaining how she used to jump off the loft into the big pile of hay on the ground when she noticed something written on one of the wooden beams in the corner of a stall. Curious, she went over to read what it said. As she got closer she realized that many years ago, when Jimmy was working on the farm, he had carved his name into the beam. Sally called her family over to see what she had found. As they came she said, "I want you to see something." She pointed to the pole and asked them to read the name carved there. It read, "James A. Garfield." At that very moment, James A. Garfield, little Jimmy, was President of the United States.

Little Jimmy, as he stood there in front of Old Man Johnson asking to court Sally, did not appear to be destined for greatness. Johnson saw a boy with hay in his hair, dirt on his shirt, and cow poop on his boots. And that is all he saw. But to truly see Jimmy, he should have looked beyond Jimmy's appearance to the inner qualities that were being formed in the young man; then the farmer would have seen the potential for greatness that was there.

Too often we look only at outward appearance. Do you see others as what they wear, what they own, or where they live? Look beyond the book's cover and observe who they really are.

Have confidence in what you will be

The young Abraham Lincoln shucked corn for three days to buy a used copy of *The Life of Washington*. After reading the book he said, "I don't always intend to delve, grub, shuck corn, split rails, and the like." "What do you want to be now?" asked his teacher. "I'll be President," the confident boy said. "You'd make a purty president with all your tricks and jokes, now, wouldn't you?" said the woman. "I'll study and get ready, and the chance will come," concluded Abe. His chance did come and he was ready—ready to lead at arguably the most critical moment of our nation's history. Lincoln saw himself as one who was destined to make an impact on his world. Although he had every reason to doubt his abilities or possibilities, he envisioned what he would be.

Be what you will be

Just dreaming of being a leader won't make it happen. You actually have to do something about it. The story is told of a man who died and went to heaven. Upon meeting St. Peter at the pearly gates the man said, "I was interested in military history all of my life. Who would you say was the greatest general of all time?" St. Peter replied, "That man over there," pointing to a person not far away. Said the inquirer with surprise, "You must be mistaken; I knew that man in life and he was nothing more than a common laborer who never did anything of significance." St. Peter replied, shaking his head, "That's right my friend. But he would have been the greatest general of all time…had he been a general." So many miss the opportunity to make a difference because they choose not to seize it. You will be a leader to the degree you have chosen to do so.

"I'm not the leader type"

Many students I have encountered quit their pursuit of leadership before they begin. They make the mistake of assuming that leadership is a personality type that is aggressive, outgoing, and charismatic. A leader may have these qualities, but these do not necessarily make someone a leader. One of the most effective leaders I have ever met was a quiet, reserved man who was faithful with the influence God gave him. You may not be the class clown, have a charismatic personality, or persuasive demeanor—but you do have influence.

Are you a born leader?

If you were to write your name on a sheet of paper and then switch your pen to the other hand and write your name again, you would find that most likely the first would be smoother and more easily done. Why is that? Is it because God made you right- or left-handed, or is it that you developed the skill of penmanship in that hand—or are both statements true? You would probably answer "both" because you were more coordinated in one side than the other growing up, but you didn't begin to write as soon as you discovered this coordination. You had to develop the skill of penmanship in that hand. Now is there such a thing as a born leader? Or is it a developed skill? Or is it both?

When you become a Christian, you receive a helper called the Holy Spirit. With the Spirit, you also take possession of a spiritual gift or gifts for the edification of God's people. Now these gifts are not some aptitude or talent you may have; rather, they are a supernatural ability to do certain works that, by yourself, you would never be able to do. You cannot drink a gallon of coffee, throw a pep rally, and get psyched up enough to do these things in your own power. They only come by the Holy Spirit's power, and the results are every bit as potent as the Source.

In 1 Corinthians 12:28, Paul gives a list of those gifts that we get at conversion. This is one of four different lists that Paul gives in the New Testament.

1 Corinthians 12:28

"And God has appointed in the church, first apostles, second prophets, third teachers, then miracles, then gifts of healings, helps, administrations, various kinds of tongues."

Let's make a list: Apostles
                        Prophets
                        Teachers

Miracles
Healings
Helps
Administrations
Tongues

Now look to the next two verses, 29 and 30. Paul uses a rhetorical style of teaching by asking questions to which the answer is obvious. He asks, "All are not apostles, are they?" and the answer is "no."

1 Corinthians 12:29, 30
"All are not apostles, are they? All are not prophets, are they? All are not teachers, are they? All are not workers of miracles, are they? All do not have gifts of healings, do they? All do not speak with tongues, do they? All do not interpret, do they?"

Let's look at our list again, crossing off those gifts that Paul mentions as not being given to every believer (note that the gift of interpretation is part of tongues).

~~Apostles~~
~~Prophets~~
~~Teachers~~
~~Miracles~~
~~Healings~~
Helps
Administrations
~~Tongues~~

You have crossed out all but *helps* and *administrations*. Why doesn't Paul mention these gifts? The reason, I believe, is because every Christian receives these two gifts. Some biblical scholars concur. Dr. Gerhard Kittle makes the following observation: "the striking point is that when in verse 29 Paul asks whether all are apostles, whether all are prophets or whether all have gifts of healing, there are no corresponding questions in respect to

51

[helper] or [administrator]."[2] He lists all but these two.

"Helps" may be translated as *service* and "administration" as *leadership*. So, we may conclude that if you are born again, you are a born (again) servant leader. The Holy Spirit deposits these gifts into the life of the Christian to build up and encourage the Church. There is always a need for leadership by godly influence and service in the body of believers, but there may not always be a need for a healing, prophecy, teaching, etc. Service and leadership are the bedrock of fellowship in a church and the most necessary to exercise.

Patience while you develop

As you are developing leadership, you must be patient. Becoming a leader does not happen overnight. An effective leader hones his skills before he needs them.

Coach Gramm was my little league football coach. By day he was an economics professor at Texas A&M University, but each evening during the fall he could be found on the fields at Tanglewood Park coaching peewee football. For years he served the kids of our community in anonymity. This period of his life helped form the servant attitude, leadership skills, and perseverance he uses today. I knew him as Coach Gramm, but you may know him now as Senator Phil Gramm of Texas. Those values he developed as a youth football coach were formed when no one cared except the kids and the parents. He may have never imagined he would serve in such a lofty leadership capacity, but he patiently did what he needed to do in order to be ready when opportunity knocked.

You need to have patience even in the midst of the most menial tasks, remembering that those chores produce leadership qualities. David was a shepherd boy before he was a king. There couldn't possibly be any job more boring and unappreciated than being a shepherd. Imagine: long hours sitting on a rock by himself in the middle of nowhere, baby-sitting some dim-witted sheep (You're probably thinking, "How do I sign up?"). David waited for his time knowing that God was in control.

Use these times you have now baby-sitting your brothers and sisters (at least they're not dim-witted sheep) to forge the qualities you need in leadership. View every responsibility you are given as conditioning for the leadership challenges ahead, and know "that he who began a good work in you will carry it on to completion until the day of Christ Jesus" (Philippians 1:6).

In Romans 5:3,4 the Apostle Paul says, "And not only this, but we also exult in our tribulations, knowing that tribulation brings about perseverance; and perseverance, proven character; and proven character, hope." Most of us don't experience tribulations in our lives on a biblical scale. But any hardship, challenge, setback, or tedious labor produces those things that will be invaluable to you when you lead.

Have realistic expectations

Many of us need to develop more realistic expectations in three key areas:

False Expectation #1

I can develop as a leader over the summer break. Leadership is a life-long pursuit that takes years of hard work and perseverance to master. God is continually working in you to form your Christlikeness and, as with me, He has a lot of work ahead of Him. But one of the great aspects of leadership is that it is a journey that is meaningful and fulfilling along the way.

False Expectation #2

My mother thinks I'm awesome so I must be. I'm sure even Judas Iscariot's mother thought he was exceptional. God has blessed us with at least one person in our lives who thinks we are the best at everything. But believing something doesn't necessarily make it true. If you are 7 feet tall, don't expect to be an Olympic gymnast.

If you can't carry a tune in a bucket, don't be disappointed if you are not asked to sing the National Anthem at the Super Bowl. You have tremendous gifting and skill potential, but keep your perspective in perspective by practicing a little humility.

False Expectation #3

Greatness in leadership means becoming President. Although we have looked at "great" (read: famous) leaders as examples, we must not discount the "greatness" that can be found in the unsung leaders all around us. You may attain greatness in leadership as a father, mother, teacher, mechanic, musician, doctor, plumber, attorney, banker, or carpenter. Leadership is found in becoming Christ-like. So if you are a man who emulates Jesus Christ, you are a *great* leader. I live in Texas (considered by the enlightened as the Holy Land) where cowboy wisdom is on a level just below Proverbs. One such nugget accurately puts this expectation in its proper place: "Generally speaking, fancy titles and nightshirts are a waste of time."[3]

At the beginning of discovering your leadership potential, you must understand that leadership is not a position, rank, or title. Too many people think that becoming a leader occurs when an authoritative person, like a king, picks us out of a crowd, commands us to kneel down before him, and touches us on each shoulder with his sword to dub us a leader. This only happens in the movies—if at all—and the truth of the matter is that you will first demonstrate leadership, and then at some point later you will receive the title of team captain, club president, officer, or leader. We must be about the tough business of leading/influencing where we are, trusting that at the right moment God will promote us to more leadership as He sees fit for His purpose. Robert E. Lee labored as a faithful lieutenant in the Engineering Corps of the US Army before he ever saw battle and won major promotions there. He measured his success not by his titles or promotions but by his faithfulness.

I remember as a boy playing catch with neighborhood friends in the front yard. I would fantasize about a major league scout passing by and spotting my throwing motion. He would then get out of his car, ask me to throw the baseball again, and with the glee of a prospector finding gold, sign me to a multi-million dollar contract. Well, it never happened. I guess the scout got lost on his way to my house. The students I talk with at Worldview Academy Leadership Camps relate a similar fantasy, hoping that someone will come along and call them a "leader" and then they will begin to lead. But this is backwards. First, I must become a great baseball player, and then scouts will recognize me. I don't become a great outfielder by being called a great outfielder.

In his book, *The Art of the Leader,* Dr. William Cohen makes this insightful observation:

> "You may have heard someone say, 'I'll wait till I'm promoted. Then I'll have an opportunity to demonstrate my leadership.' That's like the old story about the freezing man and the wood-burning stove. The man looked at the wood-burning stove and spoke these words. 'Give me heat and then I will give you wood.' You may laugh because everyone knows that you have to put wood on a fire before a fire will give you heat. The same is true about promotion. If you want to get promoted, you have to be a leader first. Then someone will promote you."[4]

Samuel Brengle was a fantastic leader for the Salvation Army. In assessing leadership he wrote,

"One of the outstanding ironies of history is the utter disregard of ranks and titles in the final judgments men pass on each other. The final estimate of men shows that history cares not an iota for the rank or title a man has borne, or the office he has held, but only the quality of his deeds and the character of his mind and heart."[5]

Don't wait around for a scout to discover you—lead now and expect the titles later. And if you earn no title other than "Mommy," remember that your children may esteem you as the greatest leader in the world. Titles may or may not follow; but great leaders realize their potential by practicing leading every day.

What you know now...

- I'm not now the leader I will become.
- Be confident that, as you are faithful, God will develop you.
- If you are born again, you are a born again leader.
- Your servant leadership power comes from the Holy Spirit.
- Be patient—God and you still have work to do.
- Have realistic expectations about your leadership.

CHAPTER THREE
Study Section

When the movie *Braveheart* hit theaters in 1993, people flocked to see Mel Gibson play William Wallace, the Scottish legend who stood up to the English in the mid-1200's. While the movie gave an accurate portrayal of the hero according to Hollywood standards, there are a few things they left out.

William Wallace was a man of large stature. During a time when the average male was little over five feet, Wallace's 6 foot 7 frame was one to be reckoned with. To complete the "fairytale-esque" picture, Longshanks, Wallace's oppressor and greatest enemy, was also a giant of a man, making the two a good match.

During those times, it was customary for the eldest son to inherit the land of his father and follow in his father's footsteps. The younger sons traditionally went to work in the church. By the time Wallace was 16, he was not only physically strong, but he was also mentally and educationally very well equipped, having spent many years under the tutelage of an uncle who was a cleric at a chapelry of Cambuskenneth Abbey. From age 14 to 17, William studied all facets of education with this uncle, from literature, to church history, to Latin and the classics. Through his study of the scriptures and other great writings, Wallace developed a deep love and appreciation for freedom and liberty, which he saw as essential to life.

When he was finally reunited with his family, everyone had high hopes for him to become influential in the church, and no doubt Wallace had that potential. But something happened to change the course of his life not long after he returned home. Longshanks, or better known as Edward I, King of England, issued an edict that every family in Scotland must pay homage to him. When William's father refused to take the oath, he and his oldest son (William's brother Malcolm) fled north into the woods. At that time, the young William became increasingly bitter toward England and their oppression of the Scottish people. When William's father was eventually killed, William vowed to avenge his death and release his people from Longshank's rule.

Now if you've seen the movie, you know basically the rest of the story. William Wallace and his rag-tag group rallied for support of the Scottish people and before long, thousands of Scots joined them to take on the English super power. Wallace was eventually betrayed and killed, but not before he made an impact on his country and on the course of history.

If you look closely at his story, you see that William Wallace was an unlikely leader. Due to his physical stature, he was looked at as somewhat of a freak of nature. He was a second son, therefore giving him few rights. And he was poor, with no money or land. For three years, while his country was in political upheaval, William was sheltered from the world as he diligently did his duties as a student and apprentice to his uncle. But it was during those three, secluded years that William Wallace learned what true freedom and liberty meant, and he developed a passion for his people.

You may feel like you too are not a likely candidate for leadership. Maybe you're too shy, or too short, or too slow, or too impatient. . . Whatever you may think, you must remember that you are not today what you will be tomorrow. All great leaders need some time to learn and grow before they can be effective. Before Paul began his missionary journeys, he disappeared into the desert of Arabia for three years, alone. Before David could become king, he sat for hours on end by himself as a shepherd watching sheep.

So what about you? What are you learning right now? And how is that going to prepare you to be the leader that God intends you to be? Reflect on this for a moment.

A Message from the Word

Moses answered, "What if they do not believe me or listen to me and say, "The Lord did not appear to you?" ...Moses said to the Lord, "O Lord, I have never been eloquent, neither in the past nor since you have spoken to your servant. I am slow of speech and tongue."
Exodus 4:1, 10

When the Lord first called him, Moses was scared and reluctant. "But Lord," he protested, "what if they don't believe me?" The Lord gave Moses three signs that he could use to prove that God had appeared to him: his staff, which turned to a snake, his hand, which turned leprous when he put it in his cloak and was healed, and the water from the Nile, which turned to blood when Moses poured it on the ground.

Despite these three miracles, Moses further protested. He was content where he was—to lead others would have been frightening and uncomfortable. But God didn't let Moses back out. In verses 14-17, God finds a solution to Moses' problem. He tells Moses to let Aaron do all the talking, but Moses was still to perform the miraculous signs. God wanted no one else for the job. He chose Moses and His decision was final.

Moses did not see himself as a leader in any capacity. He was shocked when the Lord chose him. But as you know, Moses went on to achieve great and mighty things for Israel through the Lord's power. You see, what Moses didn't understand at first was that God was not asking him to do these things alone. God had every intention of supporting and empowering Moses. God just wanted a willing vessel to carry out His wishes.

Reflection

Write down the three false expectations listed in the chapter:

1. _I can develope as a leader over break._
2. _My mom thinks I'm awesome, so I must be._
3. _Greatness in leadership means to be President_

Do you fall prey to any of these expectations? How?

I put things off and see becoming a leader as a distinct change in action. I have thought that to be a leader I have to do something big.

In what ways do you now see your potential for leadership?

Right now I hesitate, and I am lazy. But I know that I have good potential for leadership because I am willing and envision my effects

How are you willing to be used by God to accomplish His deeds?

I am willing to spend time for his will, start a small group, witness to my friends, share my personal testimony.

When Alan Hobson and Jamie Clarke decided to join an expedition to Mount Everest, they had less than two years to prepare. Mount Everest is the crown jewel of mountaineering, and many have died in an attempt to reach her summit. As part of their training, Alan and Jaime filled their backpacks with 85-90 pounds of books and water bottles, and climbed the stairs of a 29-story building everyday for three to five hours a day. They would go up and down those stairs roughly eight to ten times per day, and that was only the beginning of their training. They also ran anywhere from 15 to 25 miles per day. In order to physically make it to the summit of Everest, the dedicated men knew that they needed to be in the utmost physical shape. During their training sessions they kept one another going by constantly reminding each other of the goal and the dream that they shared.

To these two adventurers, Everest represented a peak in life that they had to cross in order to move on. Like anything that we struggle with, these two men were compelled to overcome the mountain. Though they would not reach the summit on their first expedition, they did not give up. They would return to Everest two more times before finally reaching the summit in 1997. After years of dreaming and working, they realized their dream! When he reached the summit for the first time, Alan Hobson said in a voice laden with emotion, "If there is a lesson in all of this, it is that if we persevere long enough, we can do the dreams."[6]

Preparation as a critical element of leadership cannot be ignored. And when Alan and Jaime set out to accomplish their goal, preparation filled their toolbox with the necessities for success. They prepared for a dream and, because of preparation, lived the dream. What are your leadership dreams?

I am a motivator! And so my dream is to give my family, friends and peers a view of God's goodness in the world. And do this so it reflects a better attitude and spirit of thankfulness in their daily lives.

What are some "Everest/Egypt's" in your life—those things that seem overwhelming and undefeatable?

Diabetes, bringing my family to Christ, and that's all I can think of...

Moses made excuses for his assumed inability to lead. Don't get caught in that trap! Take a few moments to list some reasons why you CAN take on a life of leadership.

I CAN take on a life of leadership because God empowers me to do so. He uses me. When it seems I don't have the words God provides them. The Lord is behind me in every step I take. It's not like I have to do it alone because I know I couldn't. Without Him. I have a voice, a heart, an attitude that Christ will use to His will.

Meekness

A LEADER

MEEKNESS

CHRIST-LIKENESS

N ow that we have a foundation for leadership, let us begin
to build skyward. Upon the base of Christ-likeness, we
will erect five pillars that will bear the weight of the
leadership life. These pillars, to my mind, are much like the
columns you might see in Athens or Rome. They are tall, straight,
well-rounded, and weather-proof—just like the character qualities they represent. Each of the pillars is dependent on the others
in that they cannot support the structure alone. If one pillar fails,
the whole structure is weakened and collapses.

These five pillars are characteristics of Jesus Christ; as you pursue
God's purpose for you of Christ-likeness, it will be necessary to
realize these in your life. Of course, there are many qualities of

Christ that you will pursue throughout your walk with God and these are only a handful of them. But, as I have observed the core characteristics of great leaders, these five are essential components for preparing to lead.

The meek shall inherit the lead

In the halls of power in politics, business, education, and sports, you will see signs, posters, slogans, and mission statements that speak of core values and vision. Leaders in these arenas stress the importance of a shared purpose in meeting the needs of the customer, providing quality products, besting their opponent, serving people, or making a profit. Often, we read words like "perseverance," "determination," "honor," and "valor." But have you ever heard the call for "meekness" in the halls of power? Can you imagine a sign in an NFL locker room that hangs between one saying "Pride" and another saying "Victory" that reads "Meekness"?

Meekness ≠ weakness

Why is meekness almost never mentioned as a core element of leadership? I believe it is because the concept of meekness is misunderstood. Unfortunately, in the English language the word "meekness" rhymes with "weakness," and our culture has attached the same meaning to each word. In reality, the two words are more like antonyms than synonyms. Weakness is powerlessness, but meekness is best defined as "controlled power." As a leader, you have influence and influence is power. When you have meekness, you simply allow that power to be controlled.

I was once in a Bible study with Dr. Bill Lawerence of Dallas Theological Seminary. He related a story about meekness that reminded me of a similar incident I had experienced. When I was growing up, my younger sister jumped horses (no, not like a motorcycle daredevil jumps buses). She rode the horses who did the jumping. You've seen the equestrian competitions in the Olympics—probably late at night during the recap show because horse jumping is one of the most boring spectator sports imaginable. Well, being a good brother dictated that I attend her events since she attended my baseball games. I remember that waiting for her to compete was the worst part of the day. I would wander around the paddock area and watch the competitors get their horses ready for the jumping circuit.

One day as I was watching one little girl prepare her horse, I saw something that I had never seen before. This little girl, only about nine years old, was saddling a Tennessee Walker. If you have ever seen a Tennessee Walker, you know that they are the Shaquille O'Neal of the equestrian world. They are massive animals with powerful features and beautiful lines. This little girl was dwarfed by the towering horse as she threw the saddle onto its back. The contrast in their sizes was striking. As the saddle landed on the horse's back, the straps and stirrups fell to each side. She reached under the animal's chest and brought the girth strap underneath and fastened it in the near buckle. What she did next made my mouth drop open in amazement. She took two steps toward the back of the horse, made a fist, and with all of her might punched the horse in the stomach. The horse gave out a pained grunt as she quickly shuffled back to the girth buckle where she drew it up a few more notches. I couldn't believe my eyes. I looked around to see if anyone else had seen the abuse I had just witnessed. Others had but didn't appear concerned. I was the only one who didn't know what she was doing.

It's a normal procedure in saddling a horse to knock the breath out to tighten the saddle. Horses are pretty smart animals and will take in a deep breath when they feel the saddle on their back. If the rider doesn't make sure the saddle is tight he could easily find himself riding underneath the horse when the horse exhales. I don't know that much about riding a horse, but I do know that it's much better to ride on top of the horse—especially when you both are jumping fences.

Eventually, the little girl mounted the horse and began to jump it through the course. This horse did everything she commanded it to do. I'm sure it would have fetched a stick or rolled over and "played dead" if she told it to. This showed me a great example of meekness. The Tennessee Walker was no less powerful, no less courageous, no less massive—yet it had direction; it had purpose. It was power under control.

The power of leadership

As you know, when you are a leader you will have power. That is the nature of leadership. Because leadership is influence, you will have the responsibility to use that power for God's purposes. You have probably heard the famous quote by Lord Acton, "Power tends to corrupt and absolute power corrupts absolutely."[1] Power without direction will corrupt the leader, the leader's institutions, relationships, and then the leadership process itself. Without this control, leadership becomes arbitrary and morphs into tyranny.

Lining the streets in your town and buried underground are electrical power lines carrying current to homes and businesses. As long as the power remains controlled by the insulation wrapping the lines, it is useful. But as soon as the control is compromised, that same power becomes dangerous and even deadly. It is the same with your power as a leader. You must allow your power to be controlled by something or someone outside of yourself—a check that makes your leadership most effective. This outside influence to *your* influence is God's plan.

A Spirit of Gentleness

In Scripture, meekness is many times rendered as gentleness. This definition is consistent with that of controlled power. To be meek is to be gentle. Gentleness is taking into account the vulnerability of others; that is, checking your power against the possibility of harming those over whom you have power. One of the most precious memories of my life is when our fourth child Gracie was held for the first time by her older brothers and sister. I remember the pre-hold coaching we gave to the kids, telling them to hold Gracie's head with one hand and to cradle her with the other close to their body. The care on each sibling's face as they took turns welcoming their new sister to the family was priceless. They were gentle with her although they had the power to squeeze her too tight and injure her tiny body. They allowed their power to be controlled for the good of their sister.

The meek Messiah

Throughout Scripture, Jesus Christ is characterized as being meek. The Old and New Testaments speak of the quality He possessed to let His power be controlled. As God Himself, Jesus had absolute power, yet He allowed His power to be directed by His Father's plan. It was His Father's purpose that He lay down His life as a sacrifice for the sins of all men. Jesus carried out this plan although He could have circumvented it. At any point in His earthly ministry, Jesus could have scrapped the whole plan and said to His Father, "Do over! Dad, let's cancel out this world and everything in it and start over. It only takes us seven days to create a world like this. Let's take a week and make another one that won't need a crucified savior." Thankfully, He didn't. He chose instead to do the will of His Father. To be sure, doing God's will can be painfully difficult, as we learn of Jesus' struggle to continue in His Father's will in Matthew 26:39: "Going a little farther, he fell with his face to the ground and prayed, 'My Father, if it is possible, may this cup be taken from me. Yet not as I will, but as you will.'" Regardless of what lay ahead, Jesus submitted to the greater purposes of His Father.

In aspiring to the goal of Christ-likeness in leadership, we should strive for this meekness. Of course in our culture of intimidation and manipulation, the temptation will be to give in and take the easy path the world has laid out. Instead, we must follow Christ's example and seek God's will instead of our own.

Meekness may seem like an imposing task, especially when doing the opposite comes naturally. But we have an ace in the hole to assist us in getting the job done. In Galatians 5:22 & 23 the Bible tells us that, "...the fruit of the Spirit is love, joy, peace, longsuffering, gentleness, goodness, faith, *meekness*, temperance: against such there is no law." Since the Holy Spirit Himself is giving us the meekness we need, all we must do is allow Him to bring it out.

Meekness and humility

There is an element of humility in meekness. Some would consider the connection between the two to be weakness. Actually the connection between humility and meekness is perspective. To lead well, you must maintain the proper perspective regarding your position in creation, your size, and your relative power to master circumstances. Obviously, when we stand silently looking up at the night sky, we can recognize our relative insignificance. When we are challenged by events beyond our control, we are made aware of exactly how dependent we are. But this perspective also requires an understanding that our abilities are a gift from God, and that our position doesn't preclude us from any service that is needed.

My good friend Todd Kent tells the story of a flight he was on not too long ago. He sat next to a pilot for the airline who was on his way to crew base to take his last trip before retirement. The pilot, a distinguished looking man with graying hair and a confident air, told Todd his plans for his last flight.

The man began his career as a baggage handler for the airline. During the years he was loading luggage onto planes, he would, in his off time, take flying lessons. He amassed hours in the air and applied to the airline's pilot corps. After some time, he was finally accepted and trained to become a commercial pilot. Beginning in the co-pilot's seat, he spent several years developing his skills. Finally he merited the left seat of the cockpit. As a captain, he flew thousands of hours without incident. Now it was time for his retirement and his last flight. As he related his story to Todd, there was a sense of pride and accomplishment in his voice, tempered by a strong tone of humility. As the plane landed at its destination, Todd thanked the captain for the interesting story. The other passengers gathered their belongings and waited for the doors to open, but Todd noticed the captain was staring intently out the window, watching the ground crew unload the plane. After a short pause, he turned to Todd and pointed to the work being done outside. He said, "You know what I'm going to do when I park my jet for the last time? I'm going to be the first one off the plane. I'm going to exit the jetway to the tarmac and help the men unload the baggage just as I began." This captain understood humility. He was no less a captain handling luggage than when he was responsible for hundreds of lives in the left seat.

To be humble is to have perspective. It is, as Rudyard Kipling put it, to "walk with kings–[and not] lose the common touch."[2] To be humble makes you no less a leader than being bold does, but in our present culture, it makes you an uncommon one.

God is in control.

"For all who are being led by the Spirit of God, these are sons of God."—Romans 8:14

A key component of meekness in leadership is to know that God is in control. He is at the helm although you may appear to be holding the steering wheel.

An old mentor of mine used to describe how the Holy Spirit works to accomplish His purposes through us. The mentor described a familiar summer afternoon scene in any neighborhood: a father mowing the front yard with his young son following behind pushing a plastic toy mower. My own son, Travis, must have been about three when he started "helping" me with the yardwork. I would crank up the lawn mower, head out toward the jungle that previously was my front yard, and Travis would follow right behind me with his toy mower. That "bubble mower" of Travis' was a fine machine; you just poured in some soapy water and he could cut the front and back yards, bubbles spewing out the top, without filling up. We must have been a sight for motorists passing by—Dad circling the yard in narrowing boxes and son right on his heels. When we finished, Mom would bring out iced tea for me and Kool-aid for Travis, and we sat on the front porch admiring a masterful job. Travis always felt an equal sense of accomplishment, and I allowed him to. The Holy Spirit works with us in the same way. He is out in front, cutting a wide swath and doing the real work, while we are following behind with our little toy mower. We complete the task together, but the job is actually achieved by the One in the lead.

General Dwight Eisenhower understood this principle. On July 10, 1943, the General watched as an armada of 3,000 war ships sailed into the night from Malta to the beaches of Sicily. Observing the formation he had ordered to battle he commented to an officer standing next to him, "There comes a time when you've used your brains, your training, your technical skill, and the die is cast and the events are in the hands of God, and there you have to leave them."[3]

Duh!

Actually, it is easy to be meek when you know just one truth—God is God and you are not. When I encounter events that are not what I would have ordered, I like to say, "When I am king—things are going to be different." Somehow I would make everything perfect.

Well, it would be different all right. If I were king, things would be a disaster! I am still trying to learn that God is God and I am not. At some point in our leadership life, we come to the realization that this is a better arrangement than the converse. Oliver Wendell Holmes Jr., when answering a question by a newspaper reporter on his ninetieth birthday, stated: "Young man, the secret of my success is that at an early age I discovered I am not God."[4] To know that you are the clay and not the potter allows you to not only be molded by the Master, but to also rest in the assurance that He has matters well under control. When you go to bed tonight, thank God that He is King and you or Randy Sims is not.

What you know now...

- There are five pillars of leadership, and meekness is number one.
- Meekness is not weakness but is controlled power.
- To be a Christ-like leader, you must be a meek leader.
- God is in control no matter what happens.

CHAPTER FOUR
Study Section

The raging Colorado River has cut a swath through the American Southwest as long as there have been mountains to feed her. Throughout the river's history it has been an untamed force that defied navigation and rejected confinement. For centuries, spring thaws and seasonal downpours upstream have turned the meandering flow into a destructive and deadly torrent. Man's desire to bring the river into subjection was not realized until the early 1900's when an ambitious dam project was proposed and eventually funded by Congress. This massive structure was to be built in a narrowing of the Black Canyon between the Nevada and Arizona deserts. Taking five years, dozens of lives, and millions of dollars, the dam was completed in 1936. Towering above the canyon floor, it stands at a height of 726 feet, is 1282 feet long, and 660 feet thick. To accomplish this magnificent structure, 4.4 million cubic yards of concrete were deposited in its frame.

Since its completion, the dam has brought the unpredictable Colorado River into submission and created Lake Mead, one of the world's largest man-made bodies of water.

"Hoover Dam has stood now for more than half a century, while all around it cities and states—in fact, an entire region—have been transformed by the revolution it sparked. Water and power, dispensed at the push of a button, have turned the "profitless locality" of the arid Southwest into America's new technological and agricultural promised land, ushering in an era of material wealth and physical comfort that was undreamed of, even by visionaries who conceived the development of the Colorado River."[5]

To be sure, the Colorado is no less powerful than before the Hoover Dam project. Its power has only been directed, controlled, and guided. It is meek.

Without restraint and direction, your power as an influencer can rage unchecked, pouring over those who look to you for leadership. Is your influence (power) directed, controlled, and guided by God's plan?

A Message from the Word

Then Jesus was led by the Spirit into the desert to be tempted by the devil. After fasting for forty days and forty nights, he was hungry. The tempter came to him and said, "If you are the Son of God, tell these stones to become bread." Jesus answered, "Man does not live on bread alone, but on every word that comes from the mouth of God.". . . Again the devil took him to a very high mountain and showed him all the kingdoms of the world and their splendor. "All this I will give you," he said, "if you will bow down and worship me." Jesus said to him, "Away from me, Satan! For it is written" 'Worship the Lord your God, and serve Him only.'" Then the devil left him, and angels came and attended him.

Matthew 4:1-4; 8-10

When Satan approached Jesus in the wilderness, he came at a time when Jesus was most vulnerable. After forty days without food, Jesus was very hungry. Hunger is a very powerful motivator. A person who is starving will often do anything for a little bit of food. Without food, our minds begin to wither—we lose focus on everything else around us. Praise the Lord, Jesus stood strong.

Although Jesus was physically famished, He was spiritually thriving. Christ definitely had the power to turn the rocks into bread, and he would have had a reasonable reason for doing it— he was hungry! But Jesus saw beyond the hunger of his flesh and the temporary refreshment Satan offered. Jesus saw God's plan— He knew where He was headed, and He did not allow Satan to deter

Him. He controlled His power in a moment of temptation, and that allowed Him to fully and mightily carry out God's plan—that is, to be a blameless and pure sacrifice. Jesus was a picture of meekness that day, and He gave us a perfect example of controlled power in temptation.

Reflection

When you hear the word "meekness" what do you think of? How is that different from this chapter's definition?

meekness makes many of us think of weakness but it really is control of power with humility and submission to God. "silent strength" gentleness. self control

How does the enemy tempt you to use your power of influence outside of God's plan?

We can be tempted with persuasion for greed,

Look up scripture pertaining to God's plan in that area. Commit two or three scriptures to memory and use those to battle the enemy of meekness.

Matthew 5:5 Blessed are the meek for they will inherit the earth.
Psalm 37:11 the meek inherit the land + live in peace.
Phillipians 2:1 Imitating Christs humility.

76

For months, Kara planned to travel from her home in the United States to the Ukraine to study the Russian language for a semester. Four months before she was supposed to leave, she applied for her passport and visa, both of which she needed in order to get in, and back out, of the Ukraine. As it came time to leave, Kara's passport and visa did not show up. When she called to find out the problem, she was told that there were some processing problems and it would be two weeks before they could mail it. She could speed up the process, they told her, but it would require a large fee. Frustrated and disappointed, Kara realized that she would miss her already scheduled flight, and she and her parents began the process of booking another flight two weeks later.

The day she was supposed to leave, Kara moped around the house, still frustrated that she was losing two precious weeks of her trip. She had been praying for this trip for a long time, and didn't understand why God was delaying it. She planned on using her time in Kiev to spread the gospel, learn and spend time in God's presence. As she turned the TV on in an effort to pass the time, she was shocked when she saw Peter Jennings on the screen giving a Special News Report. A Swiss Air flight had exploded over the ocean—there were no survivors. It was the same flight that Kara should have been on that day.

We do not know, nor can we comprehend God's ways. He knows where we are to be and what we are to be doing at every moment in our lives. We often try to manipulate situations so that they work out according to our own plans, and disaster inevitably strikes. Wait on God. Allow Him to work in your life according to HIS plan. You will be astounded at the blessings He rains down on you when you stay nestled in His loving care.

What are some *personal* advantages in allowing your power to be controlled by God's plan instead of your own?

God's plan is perfect. Who am I to carry out what I think is right if God's word tells me otherwise.

What are some advantages for *others* you influence in allowing your power to be controlled by God's plan instead of your own?

God knows everything we need. If someone needs me to help them God will put me there to carry out His perfect plan.

Are you allowing God to get the glory for your life, no matter how big or how small you feel your talents are?

I admit, that I have tried to witness to people with the idea that I will be a better person when God should have been my focus.

Take a moment to think about and list any characteristics that you feel are necessary for a meek person to possess. How many of those do you see in yourself?

A meek person should be gentle, vulnerable, controlling of their power, humble, able to view life in a different (shall I say

lower?) perspective, and able
to see that God is the
ultimate controller.
   In myself I can see
gentleness, vulnerability,
without doubt. I know
at times I know that
I neglect the ultimate
power of God and look in
myself or others for answers.
I can't say that I would
(I don't want to sound
mean but...) lower myself
to another perspective in
the mindset that I feel
that I am equal to a
baggage guy (not that
that isn't an important
position... it is) I know.

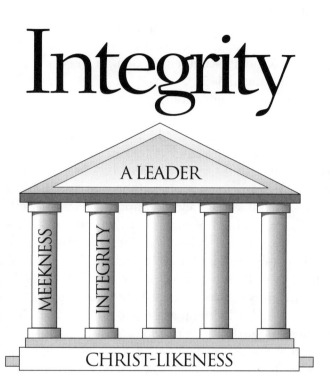

Of the five pillars of leadership, integrity is possibly the most costly. It is a quality that is increasingly rare in our culture and diluted in its meaning. Just a generation ago, integrity was an expected character quality of leadership; now it is the exception. The excuse that most modern leaders use to avoid maintaining integrity is either "higher purpose," as in "I lied to protect the innocent," or the private/public lifestyle dichotomy to which many subscribe. In a *New York Times* editorial, Billy Graham reminds us of the need for integrity both in public and private life.

"The question is asked: Why can't we just ignore personal

character, as long as a person does the job? Simply stated, it is because the stakes are too high and the impact on society too far-reaching. John Donne reminded us that no man is an island. What happens to each of us affects the whole. No leader is a moral island, either, and the greater the visibility, the greater the impact."[1]

When it comes to integrity, there is no "out" as a leader. It is prerequisite if you desire to be a servant leader.

Olympic champion Eric Liddell was a man of integrity. A portion of his amazing story is told in the film *Chariots of Fire*. Liddell was a devout Christian man who was committed to excellence, not only in athletic competition, but also in his life outside of sports. A track and field champion in his home country of Scotland, Eric earned a spot on Great Britain's 1924 Olympic team. Prior to setting sail for the Paris Games, he was informed that the qualifying heat for his event would be held on Sunday. Committed to the observance of the Sabbath, Liddell refused to run—apparently costing himself and his team a sure medal. Because of Liddell's popularity and ability, the English team committee pressed him to run, but he still declined. After realizing that this young Scotsman would stick to his guns, the committee proposed an alternate plan: Eric could change to a different event that did not run on Sunday. He agreed and began a crash training schedule for the 400-meter dash—the event for which he won the gold medal.

Eric Liddell is remarkable in that he was willing to lose the chance at international glory to remain faithful to his principles. His integrity could have cost him dearly, but regardless of the cost it had a profound impact on those around him. A fellow athlete and classmate of Liddell's, Neil Campbell, later described his decision: "Liddell was the last person to make a song and dance about that sort of thing. He just said, 'I'm not running on a Sunday'— and that was that. And he would have been very upset if anything much had been made of it at the time. We thought it was completely in character, and a lot of the athletes were quietly impressed by it. [They felt that here was a man who was prepared to stand for what he thought was right, without interfering with anyone else..."[2]]

Liddell went on to serve in the mission field in the Far East—eventually dying there in the famous Shantung Compound. He never compromised and left a legacy that continues to influence others years after his death.

Integrity hurts

Integrity doesn't always end with a gold medal. Sometimes it costs you dearly on earth. Kevin Woodrow is a name that has no significance to you, but real significance for me. Kevin was a football teammate of mine at a small liberal arts college. He was a starting defensive end and had the potential to be an all-American. But in the spring of his junior year, two things happened to him that I will not soon forget. First, he became a Christian, and then he turned himself in to the honors council because he had cheated on a test the previous semester. His infraction was known only to him and would have been undetected had he not offered the confession. As a result, he was barred from playing football that next year—the year our team won the national championship. During that season, I never heard Kevin complain or express regret for his decision to be obedient to God rather than seek the glory of man. He chose to have integrity. Integrity can cost you but in the end will be rewarded.

Having integrity also means fulfilling responsibilities even when to do so is not expected. In his book, *Up from Slavery*, Booker T. Washington describes meeting a former slave from Virginia:

> "I found that this man had made a contract with his master, two or three years previous to the

Emancipation Proclamation, to the effect that the slave was to be permitted to buy himself, by paying so much per year for his body; and while he was paying for himself, he was to be permitted to labor where and for whom he pleased.

Finding that he could secure better wages in Ohio, he went there. When freedom came, he was still in debt to his master some 300 dollars. Notwithstanding that the Emancipation Proclamation freed him from any obligation to his master, this black man walked the greater portion of the distance back to where his old master lived in Virginia, and placed the last dollar, with interest, in his hands.

In talking to me about this, the man told me that he knew that he did not have to pay his debt, but that he had given his word to his master, and his word he had never broken. He felt that he could not enjoy his freedom till he had fulfilled his promise."[3]

This courageous former slave placed integrity above comfort, convenience, and circumstance. He understood that part of being free was to accept responsibility and fulfill commitments.

I is for integrity

What is integrity anyway? Trying to define integrity is much like describing the color "red" to a blind person. It is much better understood when it is seen. I have heard it defined as when *reputation* (what people think you are) equals *character* (what you really are). But the best definition I have heard is an engineering one. It is, as Webster defines it, the quality or state of being complete or undivided. In the engineering business it is the term used to describe a building's strength and intactness. You may have visited an old abandoned farm house that was leaning to one side. As you walked through the house, stepping over holes in the floor, you were very aware of the deficiency of the structure. The building lacked integrity.

I assume that as you read this, you are inside and not sunning on the beach (although you may wish you were). As you look around at the structure that you are in right now, you probably see many things—walls, ceiling, carpet, tiles, windows, etc. Now let me ask you a question: What do you see that has something to do with the strength of the building? Most likely there is nothing that you see that has anything to do with the soundness of the structure. You are trusting in the unseen strength of the building around you: the wood studs behind the sheet rock, paint and wallpaper, the beams hidden by the ceiling, the concrete in the foundation under the carpet.

Integrity is the superstructure inside you that makes you strong, able to stand the battering of the storm. It is the character quality which makes you dependable like a strong fortress.

What's on the inside?

Several years after the sinking of the Titanic a new and grander ship was christened—the Queen Mary. She was the most luxurious ocean liner of her day and awesome in dimensions. After a long and distinguished career that spanned forty years, she was retired to Long Beach, California, to be restored as a hotel and museum. The restoration project was a massive one that included removing three imposing smokestacks to be scraped and repainted. The day came for the smokestacks to be removed by a large crane and crowds gathered on the pier to witness the impressive task. The crane cable was attached to the first of the stacks and the workers completed the job of unfastening the base plates. Receiving the "go ahead" sign from the foreman, the crane began to lift the huge stack from its fittings. The crowd applauded with delight at seeing the old smokestack begin to rise. But suddenly, the smokestack disintegrated into countless pieces. The workers ran for cover as the crowd stood silent in disbelief. The process was repeated for each stack, and each one disintegrated! Upon inspection of the remnants, it was discovered that the 3/4-inch steel plate that made up the smoke stacks had rusted away over the years, and all that was left were several layers of paint.

The Queen Mary's smoke stacks are much like the leaders of today: an impressive exterior but nothing of substance underneath. Integrity is the 3/4-inch steel plate behind your outer paint. It is unseen but crucial to your success as a leader. Dwight Eisenhower knew a lot about leadership and the importance of integrity. He once said,

> "In order to be a leader a man must have followers. And to have followers, a man must have their confidence. Hence, the supreme quality for a leader is unquestionably integrity. Without it, no real success is possible, no matter whether it is on a section gang, a football field, in an army, or in an office. If a man's associates find him guilty of being phony, if they find that he lacks forthright integrity, he will fail. His teachings and actions must square with each other. The first great need, therefore, is integrity and high purpose."[4]

Unfortunately, most of us spend much more time developing our paint, wallpaper, and carpet than we do our inner strength. To be a leader, you must begin to build the superstructure of integrity inside you, taking every opportunity to practice this rare attribute.

The good, the bad, and the dishonest

The impeachment and near-removal from office of President Bill Clinton underscores the need for integrity in leadership.

When he sinned, Clinton did not have the integrity to admit it and humbly take responsibility. This failure becomes obvious when we compare Clinton's repentance for his affair with Monica Lewinsky with King David's repentance for a similar offense. To make the contrast clear, a pastor substituted the particulars of David's sin in the text of President Clinton's address to the nation regarding his own affair. The text reads as follows:

King David's address to the nation

Good evening. This afternoon in this room, from this chair, I testified before the Office of Independent Counsel and the grand jury, headed up by Nathan, the prophet. I answered his questions truthfully, including questions about my private life—questions no Israeli citizen would ever want to answer. Still, I must take complete responsibility for all my actions, both public and private. And that is why I am speaking to you tonight.

As you know, I was asked questions about my relationship with Bathsheba. While my answers were legally accurate, I did not volunteer information. Indeed, I did have a relationship with Ms. Bathsheba that was not appropriate. In fact, it was wrong. It constituted a critical lapse in judgment and a personal failure on my part for which I am solely and completely responsible. But I told the grand jury today, and I say to you now, that at no time did I ask anyone to lie, to hide or destroy evidence or to take any other unlawful action. It was fully within my lawful powers to send her husband, Uriah, to the front lines. I know that my public comments and my silence about this matter gave a false impression. I misled people, including even my other wives. I deeply regret that.

I can only tell you I was motivated by many factors. First, by a desire to protect myself from the embarrassment of my own conduct. I was also very concerned about protecting my family. The fact that these questions were being asked in a politically inspired lawsuit, which has since been dismissed, was a consideration, too. In addition, I had real and serious concerns about an independent counsel investigation about why I wasn't at war like the rest of the soldiers. The independent counsel investigation moved on to my staff and friends, then into my private life. And now the investigation itself is under investigation, at least I hope it is. This has gone on too long, cost too much and hurt too many innocent people. Now, this matter is between me, the people I love most—my wives and Bathsheba, my new wife—and our God.

I must put it right, and I am prepared to do whatever it takes to do so. Nothing is more important to me personally. But it is private, and I intend to reclaim my family life for my family. It's nobody's business but ours. Even kings have private lives. It is time to stop the pursuit of personal destruction and the prying into private lives and get on with our national life. Our country has been distracted by this matter for too long, and I take my responsibility for my part in all of this. That is all I can do.

Now it is time—in fact, it is past time—to move on. We have important work to do—real opportunities to seize, real problems to solve, real security matters to face. And so tonight, I ask you to turn away from the spectacle of the past several months, to repair the fabric of our national discourse, and to return our attention to all the challenges and all the promise of the next Israeli century. Thank you for watching. And good night.[5]

What King David really said

Have mercy on me, O God, according to your unfailing love; according to your great compassion blot out my transgressions.
Wash away all my iniquity and cleanse me from my sin.
For I know my transgressions, and my sin is always before me.
Against you, you only, have I sinned and done what

is evil in your sight, so that you are proved right
when you speak and justified when you judge.
Surely I was sinful at birth, sinful from the time my
mother conceived me.
Surely you desire truth in the inner parts; you teach
me wisdom in the inmost place.
Cleanse me with hyssop, and I will be clean; wash
me, and I will be whiter than snow.
Let me hear joy and gladness; let the bones you
have crushed rejoice.
Hide your face from my sins and blot out all my
iniquity.
Create in me a pure heart, O God, and renew a
steadfast spirit within me.
Do not cast me from your presence or take your
Holy Spirit from me.
Restore to me the joy of your salvation and grant
me a willing spirit, to sustain me.
Then I will teach transgressors your ways, and sin-
ners will turn back to you.
Save me from bloodguilt, O God, the God who saves
me, and my tongue will sing of your righteousness.
O Lord, open my lips, and my mouth will declare
your praise.
You do not delight in sacrifice, or I would bring it;
you do not take pleasure in burnt offerings.
The sacrifices of God are a broken spirit; a broken
and contrite heart, O God, you will not despise.
In your good pleasure make Zion prosper; build up
the walls of Jerusalem.
Then there will be righteous sacrifices, whole burnt
offerings to delight you; then bulls will be offered on
your altar.

–Psalm 51

Blessed is he whose transgressions are forgiven,
whose sins are covered.
Blessed is the man whose sin the Lord does not
count against him and in whose spirit is no deceit.
When I kept silent, my bones wasted away through
my groaning all day long.
For day and night your hand was heavy upon me;
my strength was sapped as in the heat of summer.
Then I acknowledged my sin to you and did not
cover up my iniquity. I said, "I will confess my
transgressions to the Lord"—and you forgave the
guilt of my sin.

Therefore let everyone who is godly pray to you
while you may be found; surely when the mighty
waters rise, they will not reach him.

You are my hiding place; you will protect me
from trouble and surround me with songs of deliverance.

I will instruct you and teach you in the way you
should go; I will counsel you and watch over you.

Do not be like the horse or the mule, which have
no understanding but must be controlled by bit and
bridle or they will not come to you.

Many are the woes of the wicked, but the Lord's
unfailing love surrounds the man who trusts in him.

Rejoice in the Lord and be glad, you righteous;
sing, all you who are upright in heart!
                                                    –Psalm 32

Integrity against the flow

How distinctly different are the two leaders Bill Clinton and
King David. One sought to evade the truth while the latter
confessed with integrity. As a leader you can choose one of these

two routes—to have integrity or not. As G.K. Chesterton put it, "If you want to fall there are a thousand different ways but if you want to stand there is only one."[6]

Many times integrity dictates that you do what is right even though the culture or authority demands differently. Elmer Bendiner illustrates this when he describes a bombing run during World War II over the German city of Kassel.

"Our B-17 (The Tondelayo) was barraged by flack from Nazi anti-aircraft guns. That was not unusual, but on this particular occasion our gas tanks were hit. Later, as I reflected on the miracle of a twenty-millimeter shell piercing the fuel tank without touching off an explosion, our pilot, Bohn Fawkes, told me it was not quite that simple.

On the morning following the raid, Bohn had gone down to ask our crew chief for that shell as a souvenir of unbelievable luck. The crew chief told Bohn that not just one shell but eleven had been found in the gas tanks—eleven unexploded shells where only one was sufficient to blast us out of the sky. It was as if the sea had been parted for us. Even after thirty-five years, so awesome an event leaves me shaken, especially after I heard the rest of the story from Bohn.

He was told that the shells had been sent to the armorers to be defused. The armorers told him that Intelligence had picked them up. They could not say why at the time, but Bohn eventually sought out the answer.

Apparently when the armorers opened each of those shells, they found no explosive charge. They were clean as a whistle and just as harmless. Empty? Not all of them.

One contained a carefully rolled piece of paper. On it was a scrawl in Czech. The Intelligence people scoured our base for a man who could read Czech. Eventually, they found one to decipher the note. It set us marveling. Translated, the note read: "This is all we can do for you now."[7]

These brave Czechs, apparently working in a Nazi munitions factory, did the right thing even though they risked their lives to do it. Having integrity will most likely not be as dangerous as this but it certainly will, at times, mean doing unpopular things in the face of persecution and ridicule by the culture.

Honesty is the best policy (foreign or domestic)

Honesty and integrity go hand-in-hand. You cannot have one without the other. And you can't limit the scope of your honesty—it should shine in all your relationships.

Begin by being honest with God—being "real" with Him about every area of your life. Why not confess, since He knows about it anyway? This is a great place to start because it is safe. God is tight-lipped about these sorts of things and can keep your secret. Begin by practicing integrity with God.

Secondly, practice integrity with yourself. You can probably keep a secret too. Be honest about your life, choices, attitudes, and actions. Admit to yourself that you have not measured up to some of the standards which you know exist.

Now you are ready to be honest with others. I am not saying you spill your guts to everybody you meet, but you must have a commitment to truth-telling and honesty. Pledge to be up front with those you serve and lead. When someone asks you a question to which you don't know the answer, say so. If you make a report on the progress of a project that is not going well, don't sugar-coat it. If you are questioned about an incident, tell the truth. By doing this you will set yourself apart as someone who is different and worthy to be followed.

Pay now or pay later

Examples of the consequences of not having integrity in one's life are all around us. Throughout your life, if you pay attention, you will see lives lacking integrity that turn into train wrecks. One of my best friends in college was an all-conference offensive lineman for the University of Texas. He was also one of the most charismatic people I have ever known. He had the ability to rally competing interests around a common goal and a unique aptitude to communicate complex concepts that everyone could understand. I watched in amazement as kids would surround him at camps and ask him to explain the Gospel to them. He spoke to thousands and was able, in one moment, to draw uproarious laughter and in the next moment induce weeping. He was truly a "gifted" individual. I speak in the past tense because he is no longer alive. As he was leading in churches, ministries, and athletics by day, he was involved in a homosexual lifestyle and drug abuse by night. He died of what was thought to be an over-dose of anti-depressants. Although he possessed extreme amounts of personal charisma, he lacked integrity. He was never real with God, himself, or others about the critical issues in his life.

A former editor of the *Chicago Tribune*, William Bross, made this observation in an interview toward the end of his distinguished career. He was asked, "What in your observation, have been the chief causes of the numerous failures in the life of business and professional men?" He answered, "Want of integrity, careless of the truth, reckless in thought and expression, lack of trust in God, and a disregard of the teachings of His Holy Word, bad company, and bad morals in any of their many phases."[8]

If we fail to behave with integrity today, there will be difficult consequences later as our failure snowballs. Conversely, if we do the hard thing now, it smooths our path in the future. Jeff Stoddard calls this "easy now, hard later—or hard now, easy later." By doing the tough stuff now, when the failure stakes are low, we have the opportunity to hone the rough edges in our life. But waiting to develop these virtues until later may cost more than you can pay.

When my children disobey—for example, by playing golf in the living room—I will discipline them. There are usually tears and anxiety on both sides, but I know something that they do not. Correction for disobedience today is far easier than correction later when jail, divorce, or public humiliation are at stake. Know that the hard work of building integrity today will save you much in the future.

Principled leadership

Integrity in leadership also dictates that you will make decisions based upon principle rather than popularity. Most leaders today seek to win favor from those they lead by making decisions that are well-liked by the masses. Turn on the evening news on any given night, and you will hear the results of the latest poll regarding public policy.

Leadership by majority was rejected by our founding fathers for good reason. They, in their wisdom, chose a form of government that was based on principle rather than popularity. We live in a republic (rule by document—the Constitution) rather than a democracy (mob rule). Leading by polls is like an airline captain taking a vote from the passengers to see if they believe in gravity that day. Regardless of people's beliefs, there are certain things that are true now and for all time. The pilot is the leader, and as the leader he must operate in concert with certain unchanging principles.

Not long ago, former Governor of Massachusetts William Weld

was being considered by the House Foreign Relations Committee for the post of Ambassador to Mexico. Weld was a proponent of the legalization of marijuana. The committee rejected his appointment, saying that his confirmation would send a poor message to the Mexican people with regard to the United States' seriousness about fighting the drug war. The media was livid. They hammered the committee members and called the action "politically motivated." Jesse Helms, chairman of the committee, answered his detractors this way: "The American people want principled leadership—well, this is what it looks like." Helms took a beating in the press but maintained his integrity as a leader.

What are the principles that you know to be true? Primarily, of course, you find those principles in God's Word. As a servant leader you choose His principles for leadership rather than what is fashionable. Fashion changes; God's truth does not.

What you know now...

- Integrity costs.
- Integrity is the inner strength of the leader.
- Integrity and honesty go hand-in-hand.
- Lack of integrity has consequences.
- Integrity is leading by principle.

C H A P T E R   F I V E

Study Section

In 1931, a hungry seven-year-old boy from a dusty Georgia farm town stared at a box of apples outside of a small grocery store. It had been two days since the child had eaten and his stomach rumbled ferociously as he stared at the fresh produce. He waged a battle with his conscience as he looked at the inviting fruit in front of him. His parents had brought him up to believe in God's laws, and he knew that stealing was breaking one of those laws.

Suddenly, without thinking, the famished child grabbed an apple and took off running. He ran as fast as his little legs would carry him, until he reached a large grove of trees, where he sat and gulped down the apple. It wasn't long, however, before guilt set in. Once again, the small boy wrestled with his conscience, and finally, knowing what needed to be done, the young child got up and slowly made his way back to the small store.

Trembling, he approached the store owner and set the apple core on the counter.

"Excuse me, sir," he said timidly, "I took this from your stand outside and that was wrong. I want to pay you back, but I don't have any money. Maybe I could work for you after school to make it up?"

Angrily, the storeowner shooed the frightened boy away, calling him a crook and telling him to never show his face in the store again. The devastated child ran home, but told no one what happened that day. He merely decided in his own heart that he would never again break one of God's commandments. He never went back to the small store, except for one time, three days later when he sneaked out of his bedroom window late at night, and slipped an envelope containing three pennies (a gift from his grandmother) under the door of the store.

As he grew up, that little boy never forgot the lesson he learned that day. He went on to graduate from the United States Naval Academy, served as a lieutenant in the U.S. Navy, was elected to the Georgia state senate, became governor of Georgia, and in 1976 was elected the 39th president of the United States. The hungry child was James Earl Carter, Jr., a man who is known today for his lifetime of honesty and integrity in public service.

Ironically, the storeowner who humiliated the young Jimmy Carter was none other than Bruno Hauptmann, who in 1936 was executed for the kidnapping and murder of aviator Charles Lindbergh's son.

Integrity is more than just honesty. It is the notion of "what you see is what you get." Jimmy Carter does not lead a merely honest life. He leads an excellent life, striving to excel in all he does. He learned a valuable lesson as a child, and he determined to never have to learn it again. Jimmy Carter is an example of integrity in that he is his true self, whether in front of the cameras or in private. What about you? Who are you when no one is looking? Are you trying to hide who you really are from those around you, or are you truly you at all times?

A Message from the Word

"Now when Daniel learned that the decree had been published, he went home to his upstairs room where the windows opened toward Jerusalem. Three times a day he got down on his knees and prayed, giving thanks to his God, just as he had done before."

Daniel 6:10

Daniel served as an administrator to King Darius, and the king was so impressed with him that he planned to set Daniel over the whole kingdom. Daniel was a consistent and exceptional man, excellent in all that he did. His favor with the king, however, caused the other administrators and satraps to burn with jealousy. They began to look for ways to tarnish Daniel's image, but according to verse 4, "they could find no corruption in him, because he was trustworthy and neither corrupt nor negligent."

So the administrators and satraps went as a group to the king and tricked the gullible Darius into issuing a decree that commanded that anyone who prayed to any other god or man during the next thirty days be thrown into the lion's den. King Darius, obviously flattered by the "reverence" that his servants had for him, approved and issued the decree.

When Daniel heard the decree, he wasted no time in getting on his knees to pray. Note well that Daniel prayed as he had before. He got on his knees in front of his windows and prayed, giving thanks to his God! In the midst of obvious persecution, Daniel still gave thanks to his God. He changed nothing in his character, actions, or prayer time.

Well, Daniel was caught praying, and Darius, though quite distraught, had to follow through with his edict and had Daniel thrown in the lion's den. But God did not allow the lions to touch a hair on His faithful servant's head. Daniel survived his night in the den, and ultimately, those who had tricked the king paid the price not only with their own lives, but their families' lives as well.

Daniel not only had the integrity to continue to faithfully pray to his God, but he also continued to give thanks. He didn't fret over his present circumstance. He knew his God was faithful, and he trusted in that faithfulness. With circumstances shifting under Daniel's feet, he determined to exhibit the same integrity that had brought him power previously—even though it may have cost him his life.

Reflection

When people describe you, what do they say?

Young, vibrant, enthusiastic, fun to be with, friendly, warm, polite, procrastinator, motivational, smart, creative, —my parents + brother.

How would you describe yourself? Does your description match with your family and friends' description of you?

I am quiet, thoughtful, artistic, positive, a procrastinator. Our descriptions are very similar.

Have you ever acted in a way that didn't match who you really are?

Yes. Many times in class. bad example. I have something bad. When I first became a Christian I tried to pretend that I read the bible religiously. etc.

Why is integrity so important to servant leadership?

Integrity shows honesty and a compassionate leader. A leader with integrity can and will be trusted and respected by their people.

Imagine that you have the power for one day to become invisible. You have the freedom to come and go as you please without anyone knowing you are there. You can listen to any conversation without detection. Since no one knows you're there, they will talk about you freely and candidly. Would you want to hear what people say about you when they think you're not around? Why or why not?

Yes. Because then I'll know if they have integrity or not. I'd rather they tell me what they think of me to my face.

What would people say about your integrity?

There is a stopsign near my house that I don't really stop at. Otherwise I am pretty straight forward and reliable.

How has having integrity cost you in the past? What sacrifices are you making right now in order to preserve your integrity?

At my old job there were some "dirty bad" people. Since I didn't want to be part of their dirty badness I quit. I then was jobless but it ~~seems like~~ I'd rather have no job than a job where people are dirty and bad.

In preserving my integrity. I have given up friends for refusing to do bad things. (How much of a friend are they if they want me to do bad things? anyway?) I try to be a good driver. ☺. I keep my promises, help my parents, do things that I don't have to do. I don't gossip or talk about other people behind their backs. I don't cheat on homework. I stay out of other people's business.

Vision

*"I will lead the blind by ways they have not known,
along unfamiliar paths I will guide them; I will turn the darkness
into light before them and make the rough places smooth. These are
the things I will do; I will not forsake them."*
—Isaiah 42:16

"Where there is no vision, the people perish."
—Proverbs 29:18 (KJV)

*"But it is with man's Soul as it is with Nature;
the beginning of Creation is—Light. Till the eye have vision, the
whole members are in bonds."*
—Thomas Carlyle[1]

*"Give to us clear vision that we may know where to stand and what
to stand for—because unless we stand for something,
we shall fall for anything."*
—Peter Marshall[2]

The best definition of vision I have ever heard is "the ability to see God's presence, power, and plan in spite of the obstacles." It is seeing what God sees, understanding that God has chutes and ladders to circumvent any barriers or roadblocks. Vision is a "sneak preview" of coming attractions, when God allows us a glimpse of what He is going to do. It is seeing what is already there but time has not caught up to yet.

Faith and vision

The African impala is an amazing leaper. It can jump to a height of over 10 feet and cover a distance greater than 30 feet. Yet these athletic animals can be kept in enclosures with fences less than three feet tall! This is because an impala will not jump anywhere it cannot see the landing.

In some ways we are like the impala. We have the ability to leap high and cover a great distance, but we tend to shy away from unseen landings. We like to play it safe.

Vision helps stretch us. It shows us a shadow of what will be, and coupled with faith, it gives us the confidence to leap. Faith is to vision as fuel is to an engine. Faith is the quality that God gives each one of us, in different measures (Romans 12:3), which energizes our vision. We may not see the next footfall on our path, but we have confidence through faith that it will be sure.

Recently, a few men decided to unearth an old Missouri River steamship, the *Arabia*. The ship, loaded with supplies intended for frontier trading posts, struck a snag in the river and sank in 1856. The Missouri River was said to be "too thick to drink and too thin to plow" and the Arabia was quickly devoured by the Missouri's muddy riverbed. She rested there for over a hundred years while various dreamers speculated about her whereabouts. Because the Missouri's path had shifted over the years, the ship was now buried somewhere in the middle of a farmer's fields.

No one could be sure of the exact location of the ship. No one could be sure that any of the ship's cargo could survive the lengthy burial. But a few visionaries had faith that their efforts would not be in vain. The explorers obtained permission from the farm owner and borrowed money to begin the massive excavation project. Several months and $300,000 later, they had yet to uncover the first sign of the Arabia. All they had to show for their vision was a massive hole in the ground.

Imagine trying to explain to your wife (or your loan officer) that you just need to borrow a little more money to make the hole a little deeper.

Incredibly, these explorers never wavered. With financial ruin staring them in the face, they kept digging and eventually made contact with something solid and wooden. It was the steamship Arabia! With renewed enthusiasm, the crew uncovered the most complete collection of pre-Civil War goods ever discovered. Would you have kept digging? Certainly only if you were confident about your vision. Faith takes us through the times in our life when we are looking at a big hole in the ground with no victory in sight.

Seeing as God sees

A person of vision sees the "big picture." He attempts to view the world as God does. I best understand this as the difference between man and an ant. As an ant walks across a Persian rug, he only sees a horizon and what is right in front of him. But as you stand on the rug and look down, you see an ornate design. How often we are like the ant. The circumstances are all we see, yet there is a grand design and plan that God is orchestrating.

You see what you are looking for and hear what you are listening for. If you are looking for obstacles, obstacles you will see. If you are looking for opportunities, you will find them. When you receive a group picture in which you are included, who is the first person you look for? Yes, you. And you are quickly able to find yourself. In *When I Relax I Feel Guilty*, Tim Hansel writes:

> An American Indian was in downtown New York, walking with his friend who lived in New York City. Suddenly he said, "I hear a cricket."
>
> "Oh, you're crazy," his friend replied.
>
> "No, I hear a cricket. I do! I'm sure of it."
>
> "It's the noon hour. There are people bustling around, cars honking, taxis squealing, noises from the city. I'm sure you can't hear it."
>
> "I'm sure I do." He listened attentively and then walked to the corner, across the street, and looked all around. Finally on the corner he found a shrub in a large cement planter. He dug beneath the leaves and found a cricket. His friend was astounded. But the Cherokee said, "No. My ears are no different from yours. It simply depends on what you are listening to. Here, let me show you." He reached into his pocket and pulled out a hand-ful of change—a few quarters, some dimes, nick-

els, and pennies. And he dropped it on the concrete. Every head within a block turned. "You see
what I mean?" he said as he began picking up his
coins. "It all depends on what you are listening for."[3]

Are you listening for God's voice in the midst of the din of
circumstances? Are you watching for Him to make a way through
life's mine fields?

Looking for God's direction allows us to see opportunity in the
midst of difficulty. The old story is told of Jethro and Buck, two
backwoodsmen from Arkansas, who heard about a bounty of
$1000 dollars for wolves captured alive. They set out at once
tracking wolves in the Ozarks. After weeks of searching to no
avail they were exhausted and discouraged. One night, having
walked through the woods all day, they fell fast asleep under the
stars. Suddenly, Jethro awakened to the sight of a pack of thirty
wolves surrounding them with blood in their eyes and snarling
teeth. He poked his friend and said, "Buck, wake up! We're rich!"

Vision sees beyond the obvious

I won't soon forget a lesson I learned from Joe Gibbs. I was on
staff with the Fellowship of Christian Athletes in Dallas assisting
with the annual FCA Business Community Luncheon. Coach
Gibbs was on top of the world. He had just won the Super Bowl
as head coach of the Washington Redskins and was being hailed
as one of the greatest coaches of all time.

Just months after this great victory, he was invited by Coach Tom
Landry to speak at our luncheon in Dallas. Upon being introduced
to share his comments, Coach Gibbs made some perfunctory
remarks and then introduced his wife. He talked at length about her
loyalty to him and about her support through the long football sea-
sons; then he spoke about her beauty and winsomeness. At Coach
Gibbs' request, she stood, turned around, and waved to the crowd.

There was a deafening and awkward silence in the ballroom for what seemed like minutes, but was only seconds. Instead of the expected "trophy wife" common to powerful male leaders of our day, Mrs. Gibbs was scarred by a severed nerve suffered during an operation. Her face was somewhat contorted, drooping on one side as if stricken by a stroke; physically, she was less beautiful than what her husband had described. Yet to him she was indeed the most beautiful woman on earth, and her countenance showed his deep love for her. After the short pause, the crowd of men and women erupted into enthusiastic applause. The business leaders in that room understood the beauty that was hers regardless of outward appearance. It was hers because Joe Gibbs saw as God sees—a woman whom God created and loves.

To have vision is to see past the temporal and the obvious and to behold the overarching perspective of God.

Vision through the right glasses

To have clear vision you must have on the right set of glasses. You and everyone you know sees the world through a distinct pair of glasses—your worldview. Like glasses, your worldview should help you see reality clearly. If you have on the right prescription you will be able to see—if not, you will end up in a ditch. Your worldview is your framework for understanding existence.[4] It is the grid through which you filter information from your world. G.K. Chesterton said that "Insanity is not seeing reality as it truly is."[5] To see clearly and to understand the world around you, it is important to adopt the worldview that conforms to reality.

Your worldview can also be described as the foundational assumptions you make that determine your conclusions. There are two questions that make up everyone's worldview: What is the nature of God? and What is the nature of man? Everyone answers these two questions; consequently, everyone has a worldview.[6] To lead like Christ, you must answer these core questions in a way that is consistent with God's Word. Let's look at the distinct differences between how a Christian answers these questions and how the world answers them.

Depending on how you answer these two foundational questions, you will either see reality clearly or stumble through life. The clarity of your vision is determined by your worldview.

	Nature of God	Nature of man
Christian	Loving Sovereign Omnipotent Omnipresent Omniscient Just Merciful Personal	Created by God Born sinful Needs salvation Cannot please God by works Self-seeking Will be judged Has eternal soul Responsible for choices made
The world	Does not exist Arbitrary Is "out to get me" Unknowable Impersonal "force" Is everything Relentless	Evolved from lower life forms Inherently good Can become a god Is god Reincarnated Man is standard for morality Not responsible for actions

Departing from the crowd

As you begin to understand the implications of your worldview, you may become a little frightened to find yourself distanced from the false security of the majority, those who discount God's possibilities. But every great man and woman of history has at one time or another departed from the crowd.

Joshua and Caleb saw what God wanted to do for His people

and contradicted the masses to pursue that vision. When the Hebrew people, fresh from a grand tour of the desert, reached the promised land, they sent twelve "spies" into the land to see what it was like and who occupied it. When the reconnaissance group returned, they all reported that the land was lush and "flowing with milk and honey." Every spy also told of giants in the land that made the Hebrews look like "grasshoppers," and that there was no possibility of defeating them—every spy except Joshua and Caleb. These two vision-filled men agreed that there were giants but also assured the people that God had given the land to them.

In Numbers 13:30 we read Caleb's call to be faithful to the vision: "Then Caleb silenced the people before Moses and said, 'We should go up and take possession of the land, for we can certainly do it.'" You know the rest of the story. The Hebrews ignored Caleb's vision and, as a result, were forced to take some extra laps around Mount Sinai.

Your vision will be doubted, challenged, and ridiculed but, like Joshua and Caleb, you must remain committed to what God has shown you even when your sphere of influence says differently. As my old boss, Jack Turpin, said, "Legitimate leaders use their power to serve others by calling them to higher causes, tasks, and dreams than they could accomplish on their own."[7]

Find your passion

Your vision usually will be tied to your passion. God knows He didn't make robots; He doesn't ask us to constantly shun our emotions. Even when He leads you outside of your comfort zone, don't be surprised to find Him giving you a heart for that situation.

Obviously, your passion can also lead you astray. If your vision is based on your passion for wealth, power or fame, you won't be moving toward the right goals. But if you maintain the proper worldview, then your passion generates both the motivation and the perseverance to follow your vision.

Ironically, those who focus their passions on wealth don't even always achieve that temporal goal. A study was conducted of 1,500 people to track their career progress. They were divided into two groups: Group A, 83% of the sample, chose the career path that was to bring the most money at the earliest time so they could pursue what they wanted to do later; Group B, the remaining 17%, pursued a career that they enjoyed and were passionate about. After 20 years, 101 of the 1,500 had become millionaires. And of the millionaires, all but one was from Group B!

As you seek the vision that is tied to your proper passion, you will see success in ways you cannot imagine. Of course, I am not saying you will become a millionaire, but funny things happen when you are motivated by passion.

What is your passion? How does God want to use you? How is He preparing you through life experiences and training? What are you gifted in? These are just some of the questions that you must answer to begin discovering your personal vision.

The vision stroke

In sports such as hockey, golf, tennis, and baseball, an efficient and accurate stroke is crucial. Players spend countless hours of repetition perfecting their swing. The great players have perfected their stroke by doing it right over and over again. Vision is the same. The more you are aware of God's plan in process around you, the more you will begin to have a vision for where He is going and what He is accomplishing.

Can you identify what is below?

It probably wasn't too difficult to decipher the word "VISION." But how could you see it with only the middle third of the word visible? Because you have seen these letters of the alphabet so many times that your mind, through repetition, completes each one with little effort. In the same way, the more we see God's character and will at work around us, we are able to see the completed work.

Let's consider how this might work in a practical way. You have just been elected president of a student club. You are ready to take the reigns of leadership, and then everything begins to fall apart. The time commitment for being president is much more demanding than you had anticipated, the club officers are not interested in leading from their positions, the sponsor of the club decides that the club should change its purpose and focus, and you come down with the flu. All of this in the first week after taking office! At this point anyone would be wondering what God is trying to do. Is He mad at you? Does He want someone else at the helm? Should the club continue at all? By understanding God's nature and His ultimate will for Christians—Christ-likeness—you can conclude that He is teaching you that characteristic of Christ that is perseverance. You see past the "messing" of your circumstance to the "blessing" of knowing God's perfect plan.

"Altared" vision

The altars in your life are a key component of your vision. Throughout the Old Testament, the leaders that God appointed placed altars along their journeys to commemorate significant events and "big wins" where God came through for His people. These altars had names such as "God is my banner" and "Mighty God of Israel." Each altar had a special meaning to remind the people of God's faithfulness when all appeared lost.

My wife, Amy, is a champion at building altars. Whenever God answers a prayer, comes through in meeting a need, or provides protection, she writes it down in her journal. At those times when she is struggling with doubt or discouragement, she will go back through the long lists of God's accomplishments. She is a woman of vision, and her vision is strengthened by her altars.

All leaders have times of doubt, fear and anxiety. These strong feelings come with a lie that says, "Although God has come through every time up to now, maybe this will be the time He doesn't." There will be many times when things seem to be going wrong and the vision God gave you seems hopeless. At these times, as the Hebrew fathers did and Amy does, it is helpful to recall those times when God accomplished what He said He would. A good way to do this is by building altars as a reminder of God's faithfulness. You don't have to pile up rocks and sacrifice a bull, but you can write those victories down, keep a momento of the event, or maybe even compose a song or poem. And the next time things are looking bad for your plans and it appears God has taken the day off, you can look back at your "altar" and be reminded and encouraged by His past faithfulness.

Give vision

As Caleb demonstrated, leaders who can really move people must not only have vision themselves—they must pass it on to those they lead. In Habakuk 2:2, God told the prophet to "Write the vision, and make it plain upon the table, that he may run who readeth it."

Recently, I received a letter from Jim Horn, one of our summer staff members at Worldview Academy, who related his vision for leadership that God had given him at West Point. As he wrote about the need for leaders to understand what they believe as well as imparting a clear vision, he made a very perceptive statement: "Blind followers quickly turn into deserters if their eyes are not opened to see the path they have happened to take."

During the VietNam War, desertion and insubordination were

more common than in any previous American war. One possible reason is that a clear vision was never given to the troops who bravely fought on behalf of freedom. In the day-to-day conflict on the front line, there was no clear goal—much less a reason to die. Indeed, "where there is no vision, the people perish." Make your vision unmistakable to your team. Father Theodore Hesburgh once said, "The very essence of leadership is you have to have a vision. It's got to be a vision you articulate clearly and forcefully on every occasion. You can't blow an uncertain trumpet."[8]

Double vision

You can convey your vision best by giving "double vision." First, communicate a picture of the completed product: *what the end result of the mission will look like.* Churches often accomplish this by displaying a scale model of new buildings under construction. These scale models suggest a concrete hope, thereby, energizing church members.

But this isn't enough. You must also provide a vision describing *how the end will be accomplished.*

No successful sports team enters a contest without a game plan. The vision for victory is established and then the strategy to achieve victory is revealed to the team. On football teams, this comes in the form of a game script. Football coaches will script the first twenty or so plays in their team's game plan and thoroughly rehearse them with the team. The team will then have a vision of how they plan to reach the goal of winning, at least for the first twenty plays. You, as a leader, will impart a game plan in the same way. What are the steps that need to be taken to accomplish the overall vision?

This aspect of the vision is on a strategic level more than a tactical one because there are many variables in any venture that God can manipulate. Adjustments are made to the game plan depending on the circumstances. A coach will alter the game script based on the alignments, adjustments, and tactics of the opponent. So too, you will carefully observe the unfolding circumstances surrounding the vision and make appropriate changes to effectively navigate through the uncharted waters.

There are many ways to accomplish this double vision. Jesus chose to give vision to us and His disciples through parables. He used common images around His team to teach truths about the Kingdom. How could these mere men comprehend such sublime concepts? Jesus used stories to help them see. He drew a picture in their minds of what the Kingdom looked like (completed product) and how it operated (game plan). And when their time came to lead, they were, through the enlightenment of the Holy Spirit, able to impart the truth of the Kingdom of God to others.

Trust

"You get the most out of people by putting them in an environment where you don't have to pull their best out of them, but where they want to give it. If the leader is competent and a person of honor, others will trust the person to go around the corner, knowing the leader will take care of them and help them be successful." [9]

- General Colin L. Powell USA (Ret.)

We trust those we believe in, who have a better view, and who have demonstrated trustworthiness in the past.

Learning to swim is sometimes a traumatic experience for little children. Jumping into the water from the side or diving board can be like jumping out of an airplane. When my daughter Stacy was learning to swim, we would go to the pool, and she would cling to me as we waded around the shallow end. As time passed, she got brave enough to jump to me from the diving board. I would tread water under the board as she crept to the edge.

Holding out my hands, I would tell her to jump when she was ready. She would ask me, "Daddy, what if you don't catch me?" I would respond with, "You can do it; I'll catch you every time." She finally jumped and guess what? I caught her. She would look at me so pleased with herself and want to go again and again. And each time I caught her. The trust that she displayed was built over many experiences we had together where I had been faithful.

In this way, those who catch your vision need to know you can be trusted to catch them. And that trust is built through your being worthy of trust as a leader.

What you know now...

- Vision is the ability to see God's presence, power, and plan in spite of the obstacles.
- Vision is seeing as God sees.
- Your worldview determines how you will perceive reality.
- Building altars provides encouragement.
- A leader not only has vision but also gives vision.
- Double vision is seeing the completed product but also laying out how it may be done.

CHAPTER SIX

Study Section

When John Gutzom Borglum was a child, he determined that he would someday be important. Growing up in the late 19th century, without a father, Borglum was a quiet child and deeply creative. At the age of 16, he left his family and set out to make a name for himself in art. By his early thirties, Borglum was recognized as one of the most talented artists of the time. His sculptures were in museums around the world. He even sculpted a bust of Lincoln that Teddy Roosevelt displayed in the White House.

In 1915, Borglum was hired to carve a monument to the confederate soldier in the side of Stone Mountain in Georgia. The project would be short-lived due to funding and other mishaps, but that event ignited Borglum's dream of mountain carving. At 57 years old, Borglum found his calling. He determined to create the "eighth wonder of the world" in the side of a mountain. He had only one problem. Where to build it.

Around that time, the Governor of South Dakota contacted Borglum about the possibility of carving a monument in the side of Mount Rushmore. Racked with poverty, South Dakota desperately needed something that would bring tourists in. Borglum visited the mountain and said "yes" almost immediately. Standing at the bottom of Mount Rushmore, Borglum could plainly visualize former Presidents George Washington and Abraham Lincoln in the jagged rock. The longer he stood there, the more his vision grew. He would also add Jefferson and Roosevelt.

Borglum proposed his idea and was immediately met with sharp criticism and scorn. He became a national joke and was called a fool for thinking it could be done. Not only was he ridiculed outside of the state, but inside the state he ran into trouble as well. The matter of funding was tricky as South Dakota had very little to give. But Borglum would not be swayed. He pursued other options and finally hit the jackpot. The senator of South Dakota, a millionaire named Peter Norbek, saw Borglum's vision and agreed to help him get support from the government. Almost two years after he first envisioned his dream, Borglum went to work carving George Washington in the side of the white cliff.

The challenges of such a massive endeavor were great. For fourteen years, Borglum and his crew battled horrendous conditions. Every day the men hung precariously over the 500-foot cliff drilling holes into the tough granite. Though they worked through vicious dust storms, high winds, and even the depression of the early 1930's, which required them to abandon the project for a few months, the men pressed on. Borglum's laborers caught his vision.

Despite the setbacks, Borglum is constantly remembered as saying that workers had to be courageous. He urged them to fight through the difficulties and always brought them back to the vision.

In 1941, when the project was nearly completed, Gutzom Borglum passed away—he was 73 years old. Today, Mount Rushmore is still in the state that it was in when Borglum died. Borglum did indeed accomplish his vision—Mount Rushmore is one of the "wonders of the world," and it is revered as one of the great American symbols of freedom.

A Message from the Word

Then I said to them, "You see the trouble we are in: Jerusalem lies in ruins, and its gates have been burned with fire. Come, let us rebuild the wall of Jerusalem, and we will no longer be in disgrace." I also told them about the gracious hand of my God upon me and what the king had said to me. But when Saballot the Horonite, Tobiah the Ammonite official and Geshem the Arab heard about it, they mocked and ridiculed us. "What is this you are doing?" they asked. "Are you rebelling against the king?" I answered them by saying, "The God of heaven will give us success. We his servants will start rebuilding, but as for you, you have no share in Jerusalem or any claim or historic right to it."

Nehemiah 2:17-20

Nehemiah was a man of great vision. When he heard that Jerusalem still lie in ruins, he wasted no time in taking action. But one man could not rebuild the massive walls alone—he needed help.

Nehemiah was an excellent motivator, planner and organizer. That, coupled with his consistency, persistence and faithfulness in prayer made him quite a leader. He used his God-given talents and strengths to accomplish one of the greatest construction feats of all time. But Nehemiah didn't just wake up one morning and decide to rebuild the city walls. At the time that God called him, Nehemiah wasn't even living in Jerusalem. He lived in Persia. When he received the news that the city walls of Jerusalem remained in ruins (they'd been destroyed nearly thirteen years earlier), it broke Nehemiah's heart. As he knelt down and spoke with his Lord, a vision began to form in his mind. Nehemiah chose to accept this "impossible mission," and he set out on his own in obedience to God's call.

When he arrived in Jerusalem, Nehemiah received anything but a warm welcome. He was a foreigner, he had no money and no power. But Nehemiah was secure in himself and in his vision. He had been highly favored by the Persian king Artaxerxes (say that three times fast), whom he served as a cupbearer. Nehemiah also spent hours on end in prayer where his vision matured.

As Nehemiah rallied for help, he slowly found supporters, and together they began to rebuild the fallen walls. It didn't take long, however, for Israel's enemies to begin pointing fingers and mocking the "foolish" Israelites. But as the builders continued in their work backed by Nehemiah's encouragement and vision, their mockers were quickly put in their place. You see, a vision from God, when carried out in full obedience, cannot fail! The wall of Jerusalem was rebuilt in record time, and with the completion of the project, God used Nehemiah to bring about a spiritual awakening among His people.

Prayer is vital to vision. Where will you get the vision if you are not on your knees? Learn from Nehemiah's example. Follow the Lord's guidance and as you go, bring others with you so together you can bring about spiritual awakening wherever you go!

Reflection

Do you have a sense of vision for what God wants you to do in life? What is that vision?

> I think God wants me to motivate, encourage and inspire. These things seem to be something I'm pretty good at.

Do you know someone whom you could describe as a person of vision? What makes you see that person in such a way?

> My Grammy Vikki is a true visionary. She always has a picture in her mind of a goal for charity work or organizing in her church. What makes her so awesome is that she follows through.

What do you see as the biggest obstacle in living a life of vision? Why?

Failure. Sometimes I fear that my vision is worthless or so easily crushed.

What is your passion? How has God gifted you to pursue this passion?

My Passion is to make people smile and see the good in all that God has given us.

When Reverend Billy Graham began his now famous crusades, he kept company with a few dear friends who encouraged and challenged him. One of those friends was John Boten, a former German industrialist who had once acquainted himself with Hitler. When Hitler's true nature became evident, however, Boten broke ties with him and came to the United States where he committed his life to the Lord at one of Graham's crusades. A man of passion, who had a desire to learn, Boten quickly developed an encyclopedic knowledge of the Bible as he studied it daily. He also became a man of fervent prayer, spending hours daily on his knees.

Billy Graham is known as the greatest preacher of our time. Millions have come to Christ through his magnificent teaching, and multiple U.S. Presidents have benefited from his advice. What many may not know, however, is that when Graham first started out, he came very close to quitting his evangelistic mission and just settling down to pastor a nice, small church.

In his autobiography, *Just As I Am*, Reverend Graham remembers talking to Boten about his concerns. He admitted to his friend that he didn't feel comfortable in the spotlight. The nation-wide attention unnerved him, and he told Boten that he thought he would rather just be a pastor. Boten's response, however, opened Graham's eyes to the vision and plan that God had for him.

"Billy," Boten said, "I can envision you preaching in the great stadiums of the capitol cities of the world. I believe the world is ripe and ready to listen to a voice of authority like yours. They are in need of the Gospel. You are the man to give it to them."[10]

John Boten saw the Lord's plan for his friend. God gave him a vision for Reverend Graham, and Boten did not hesitate to speak this vision into Graham's life. Praise God that he did!

Not only are you to act on the vision that God gives you for yourself, but you are to also encourage those around you to accomplish their dreams and passions. Remember, a quality of a good leader is to build up other leaders. Don't be afraid to encourage vision in a friend's life if you feel led by the Lord to do so.

How have you seen your intimacy with God affect your ability to have vision?

When my focus is on God I know that I keep looking for what he wants me to do and then I have the biggest urge to jump up and do it.

Share a vision with your parents, a close friend, or a leader/teacher/pastor and ask them to give you feedback on how it could come to pass. Write down their responses below.

I talked to a friend about how I wanted to impact people by motivating, encouraging

and sharing my testimony
with them so that I
may show them to be
thankful and joyous in
every situation because
God has a perfect
plan and does so much
for us. My friend told
me to ~~talk~~ (as well as
keep on encouraging others)
talk to my small group about
doing the same thing,
Speaking in youthgroup or
Chapel, or go into detail
about it in a devotional
at school.

Attitude

"Your attitude should be the
same as that of Christ Jesus…"
—Philippians 2:5

"Pessimism in our time is infinitely more
respectable than optimism. The man who sees the decline
in juvenile delinquency is a negligent, a fool and a foolish fellow.
The man who foresees catastrophe has the gift of insight
which will assure that he will become a famous
radio commentator, the editor of
Time Magazine or go to Congress."[1]
—Viktor E. Frankl

To be a servant leader who is not only worth following but also admired, you must maintain the proper attitude. Those you influence through leadership will be energized or discouraged by your attitude.

During the American Revolutionary War, the colonists were faced with the task of defeating the most powerful military force on the face of the earth. This rag-tag band of militias armed only with hunting rifles and outdated weaponry were outnumbered and outgunned in every way. They had the opportunity to give in to negative defeatist attitudes but instead chose the converse. Led by the positive attitude of George Washington, they saw their relative lack of size as an opportunity. While the British were big and slow, they were small and mobile. The British were well-organized, but they were free to strike at anytime. The British were professional soldiers, but they were fighting on their home turf and knew the terrain. What could easily have been defeat was turned to victory by focusing on strengths rather than weaknesses.

To have a positive, proactive, joyful attitude is not ignoring negatives in the leadership process but rather choosing the upside of any circumstance. It's focusing on the positive rather than the negative.

In determining whether to have a positive or negative overall attitude, you are deciding the environment in which you will lead— an atmosphere of joy or one of defeat, fear, and depression. By choosing a positive overall attitude, you will see possibilities and opportunities, and those you lead will sense the same.

Chuck Swindoll writes,

"The longer I live, the more I realize the impact of attitude on life. Attitude, to me, is more important than facts. It is more important than the past, than education, than money, than circumstances, than failures, than successes, than what other people think or say or do. It is more important than appearance, giftedness, or skill. It will make or break a company, a church, or a home. The remarkable thing is that we have a choice every day regarding the attitude we will embrace for that day. We cannot change our past. Nor can we change the fact that people will act in a certain way. We also cannot change the inevitable. The only thing that we can do is play on the one string we have, and that is our attitude. I am convinced that life is 10 percent what happens to me and 90 percent how I react to it. And so it is with you – we are in charge of our attitudes."[2]

Our leadership is in direct proportion to the attitudes we pursue and possess.

Do you have an attitude?

Pastor John Maxwell conducts an exercise during his seminars that I have used with some modification at Worldview Academy Leadership Camps. Let's try it. Think of a person you admire—

someone you would like to be like, someone who has had a great influence in your life. Now list the qualities of that person you admire most—qualities that you would most like to have displayed in your life, characteristics you would like to have in your own package. Your list will probably include one or more of the following:

Leadership. patience kindness

faithful	integrity	courageous	*forgiving*
truthful	godly	trustworthy	*thankful*
loyal	good listener	committed	*positive*
persevering	*honest*	loving	*intelligence*

Aencouraging. Shumor giving. rebuking. accountable

You may want to add your own to the right column. Now grade each attribute by marking with an **A** those that have to do with attitude, an **S** those that have to do with skills, and an **L** those that refer to looks. How many of these that you listed are attitudes? My guess is that most of them are. You probably didn't list many (if any) qualities that had to do with physical beauty, talents, skills, or possessions. I think that it is interesting that what we know about Jesus has most to do with His attitudes. We don't know what He looked like, what color of clothes He wore, or if, he was talented in music or sports. What we do know about are His attitudes—the same attitudes we are called to display.

It is also interesting that the qualities we admire most in others are in the category upon which we spend the least amount of time. What percentage of your day do you spend on your looks (buying clothes, grooming in the mirror, brushing teeth, picking out what to wear, thinking about how you appear to others)? What percentage of your day do you spend on developing skills (schoolwork, job, music, athletics)? And what percentage of your day do you spend developing your attitude? I would imagine that if you were honest with yourself, you would find that your priorities are skewed.

proverbs.

Making an attitude adjustment

So how do I get attitudes like those of the people I admire most? These virtues are developed in two ways: first, by meditating on them in God's Word; and second, by hanging around people that practice and value these virtues.

The grinding work of cud chewing

The first step toward developing the attitude you desire requires spending time with God. By meditating on the character qualities of the great men of faith, and primarily on those of Jesus Christ, you will begin to value those same attitudes in your own life. In Joshua 1:8 we read, "This book of the law shall not depart from your mouth, but you shall meditate on it day and night, so that you may be careful to do according to all that is written in it; for then you will make your way prosperous, and then you will have success." (NASB)

The word "meditate" is best pictured as a cow chewing the cud. To eat, a cow will take a bite of grass or hay, chew on it for awhile and then swallow. Really amazing, you say. But what it does after that is different. The cow will toss the food back up from the stomach into the mouth to chew on it some more and then swallow again. This process will go on for some time in order for the cow to digest it. We are to do the same thing with God's Word. Read a passage, put it down, go about your business, think about it again, do something else, think about it some more, and so on.

The good and bad of company

The second way to acquire the proper attitude is by hanging around those that practice what they preach. I cannot emphasize enough the inevitability of your friends' attitudes rubbing off on you. As Paul wrote in 1 Corinthians 15:33, "Do not be misled:

'Bad company corrupts good character.'" You have seen it before. A friend who used to be a close one begins to run around with the "wrong crowd," and before you know it he is a different person, changed by his peers. You may have also seen it in your own life. Peer power is one of the most potent cause-and-effect laws in our nature. Make sure you are witnessing daily those attitudes you desire.

Working for the Fellowship of Christian Athletes in Little Rock, Arkansas, was an eye-opening experience for me in many ways. As part of my responsibilities, I chaperoned a group of inner-city teens to an FCA summer camp (I later found out that these guys were all in a gang.) I rented a van and picked them up at the designated sight for the trip to Texas. The demographics of the van trip were one white boy, me, and nine black youth. Our trip was uneventful and quite educational for me as I learned new lingo and forms of music from the tapes they brought. It must have been pretty comical to the "gang" as they heard me try to repeat a rap song they taught me. I got to hear about the students' lives, families (if any), favorite sports teams and heroes.

One student in particular, named Demarcus, who seemed to be the head man of the group, was open and warm in his conversation. Demarcus didn't know who his father was, but he was close to his mother who had raised him and his nine brothers and sisters.

We arrived at the camp, and each student was assigned a roommate and small group. We hadn't been there three hours when one of the college counselors frantically approached and told me that one of the kids I brought had pulled a gun on his roommate and threatened to kill him. I was used to dealing with pillow fights at camp; this was a new challenge.

We went to the student's room where he was being kept by some of the other staff members until I arrived. When I walked in, I was shocked to see Demarcus sitting on the edge of his bed with his head down. He looked up at me, and I could sense the anger in his eyes. The staff members left us (except for one), and I asked

Demarcus to explain what had happened. He went through the story of how his roommate had made a comment about his basketball shoes being better than Demarcus', and it escalated from there.

Demarcus and I talked candidly for the next two hours about expectations, teamwork, and his attitude. As we talked about attitude, Demarcus had a look of puzzlement on his face, as though I was speaking Portuguese. I asked him if he could tell me in his own words what a Christ-like attitude meant, and he couldn't. He didn't have the foggiest notion of what it could be. I asked if he knew anyone who was consistent in acting like what he thought Jesus would act like, and he answered that he didn't. I explained, as best as I could, what that attitude was and how important it was in his maturation. As we talked, I could tell that his heart was softening, and the hardened exterior was cracking. After we prayed together, he looked at me with tears in his eyes and said, "Mr. Randy, why hasn't anybody ever told me about attitude?" I wasn't able to give him an answer. Demarcus had a problem that was much greater than being in a gang—his greatest problem was that he had no one to observe demonstrating a Christ-like attitude on a daily basis.

Your attitude will be determined by those you observe much more than you realize. So choose your "gang" carefully.

Your attitude indicator

A friend of mine is a corporate pilot for a major U.S. company. We were discussing the concept of attitude one day when he made an interesting observation. He told me that the attitude indicator on an airplane is the most important piece of equipment for the pilot. It is the instrument that has an artificial horizon with the silhouette of a plane superimposed on it. From reading this, the pilot can determine where the plane is in relation to its surroundings. All of the other navigational equipment are secondary to the attitude indicator. He told me how, by focusing on the attitude indicator during confusing surroundings and zero visibility, the pilot can fly through virtually any weather.

What is the "attitude indicator" in our life? It can be one of many things that let us know if our attitude is correct. I believe the primary instruments for us is God's Word, our authority figures, and our friends and family. These will give a "true" reading of our attitude. I remember a time when I was playing baseball in college. My roommate was the catcher for the team, a friend, and a Christian. During the season, my attitude began to deteriorate as I picked up those attitudes of the baseball team. I was completely unaware of this shift. One day after I had expressed my attitude about a situation on the team, my roommate pulled me aside and brought it to my attention. I was shocked at how right he was and how blind I had been to the change in attitude. By observing my attitude indicator, in this instance my friend, I was able to correct my bearing. God's Word tells us in Proverbs 27:6, "Faithful are the wounds of a friend; but the kisses of an enemy are deceitful." A friend or family member is sometimes the only one who will tell us the truth about ourselves. And, as scripture tells us, it is better to be set straight by a faithful friend than to be told we are "looking good" by an enemy.

Attitudes can make or break you

Attitudes are determined by you, and then they determine you. A bad attitude begets a bad destiny, and likewise, a good attitude begets a bright destiny. I'm not talking about getting out on the wrong side of the bed; I'm talking about attitudes that are life-long and life-changing.

George Washington Carver, one of America's greatest scientists and educators, once said,

"Fear of something is the root of hate for others, and hate within will eventually destroy the hater. Keep your thoughts free from hate, and you will have no fear from those who hate you. David, though small, was filled with truth, right thinking, and good will for others. Goliath represents one who let fear into his heart, and it stayed there long enough to grow into hate for others."[3]

An attitude like hate can and will eventually corrupt the person who embraces it. So too, any attitude that contradicts God's principles and purpose will also be a cancer to the servant leader.

Attitudes dictate actions

At the beginning of any action there is an attitude. To forgive you must have a forgiving attitude, and to serve you must first have a serving attitude. Jesus knew the powerful consequences of attitudes. In Matthew 5:27-28, He says, "You have heard that it was said, 'You shall not commit adultery'; but I say to you that everyone who looks at a woman with lust for her has already committed adultery with her in his heart." He was teaching that attitude and action are inextricably linked. Jesus calls us all to combat sin at the attitude level and produce good works by cultivating Christ-likeness at the same level.

The attitude of Christ no matter what

One of the most tragic disasters in the history of aviation occurred in the skies over Lockerbie, Scotland. Pan Am flight 103 exploded in mid-air with 243 passengers and 16 crew members aboard. A terrorist's bomb had been detonated in the cargo hold, effectively ripping the 747 into six sections at 31,000 feet. The splintered remains of the jumbo jet, cargo, and passengers plunged to an area 40 miles wide in and around Lockerbie, a town of about 3,000 people.

The town received extensive damage and eleven townspeople were killed by falling wreckage. The debris was everywhere, and corpses littered the countryside. What was once a peaceful farming community was now abuzz with an international effort to investigate the crash site. Security was tight, and most of the area allowed access only to locals. Mourning for the victims was a worldwide event and was followed by outrage. Families of the victims attempted to enter the crash zone but were turned back by international security forces patrolling the perimeter.

The people of Lockerbie felt helpless to do anything for these families, but they eventually began the small service of collecting articles of clothing from victims and sorting them. Then they washed and pressed each article to look as fresh as possible. They asked for permission to return the clothes to the families, and it was granted. This small service profoundly impacted the victims' families, who were touched by the humble people of Lockerbie who themselves were mourning their own loss.

Imagine the opportunity those Scots had to choose their attitude. They had lost loved ones, homes, businesses, their way of life, and witnessed a horrible disaster. Yet they chose to serve, to display an attitude of compassion, and to be Christ-like. And their attitude blessed those they touched and those beyond their reach.

As a leader, you will have many opportunities to choose your attitude. How you choose will make all the difference in your success as a leader. And it is a choice!

What you know now...

- Attitude is what you admire most in other leaders.
- Your attitude is shaped by what you meditate on and who you are around.
- We get feedback on our attitude from God's Word, authority figures, and friends and family.
- Attitude can make or break you.
- Choose your attitude now, before the disasters arrive.

CHAPTER SEVEN
Study Section

September 11, 2001, is a day that none of us will ever forget. It is forever ingrained in our minds as one of the greatest tragedies in American history. We will talk about it for years to come, remembering where we were and what we were doing the day terrorists attacked the United States.

Not to be forgotten either is the way that Americans pulled together. For a rare time, Americans put their differences aside and joined in prayer, mourning and spirit to remember those lost in New York City, Pennsylvania, and Washington, D.C.

Throughout the course of this book, we have been studying the incredible power of leadership, and in the wake of the attacks, we saw this type of leadership played out before our eyes. President George W. Bush seemed an unlikely candidate when he first announced his bid for the presidency, but after a tight and much publicized election, he took office. He had no idea that he would be the President during "such a time as this," but God did. While Bush seemed to have the potential for leadership before, he emerged as a truly great leader during a time of crisis.

Throughout his candidacy and Presidency, Bush never withheld from the public his religious beliefs, and during times of turmoil, his faith in God continued to keep him strong. A few weeks after September 11, the President met with some of the great preachers from around the nation for breakfast and prayer. During this meeting, the pastors and teachers were shocked at Bush's energy and positive attitude. When asked how he could be so energized and positive, Bush replied that his attitude could only come from God empowering him through the prayers of the country.

After September 11, our "normal" way of life suddenly seemed petty and selfish. In an issue of TIME Magazine printed just before the attacks, the headline article dealt with the anniversary of the Bush/Gore election. A large rally was being planned in Florida in protest of the outcome of the November, 2000, election. It was to be a huge demonstration with important people from all over the country scheduled to speak. At the time, this "big news" seemed important and justified.

All those feelings of resentment changed, however, on that frightening Tuesday morning. It no longer mattered what happened the year before. Suddenly, the entire nation's attitude changed from selfish bickering to commitment, truth and justice. The American flag was once again a staple on cars, homes and clothing. As we pulled together trying to make sense of this tragedy, we desperately needed leaders with an "attitude like that of Christ Jesus." We needed people to stand up and fight for each other, rather than fight for themselves. We needed someone who was willing to take risks and who was firmly rooted and established in the love of Christ. We needed godly men and women to stand up and lead.

So how about it? Will you be one of them?

A Message from the Word

Finally brothers, whatever is true, whatever is noble, whatever is right, whatever is pure, whatever is lovely, whatever is admirable—if anything is excellent or praiseworthy—think about such things. Whatever you have learned or received or heard from me, or seen in me—put it into practice. And the God of peace will be with you.

Philippians 4:8-9

So how do you have an attitude that lifts the spirits of a nation? It starts with meditation. Reread the verse above. Look at what Paul urged the Philippians to think about—truth, honor, nobility, loveliness, excellence, etc. Paul knew that attitude came from within. When your mind is on the slasher movie you and your friends saw the night before, or someone you are angry at, or anything else of the "unpositive" nature, then your attitude will reflect that. The reason that President Bush could have such a positive attitude is because he did not dwell on the tragedy. Instead he looked for the good, and he urged Americans to do the same. This attitude bolstered our spirit in a time when we definitely needed it!

The second thing that Paul urged the Philippians to do was to model themselves after him. Christ-likeness comes from observing others who are Christ-like. As you observe someone that you admire, notice the things that they talk about. How does their attitude reflect what they think? Spend time with that person and listen to their words of encouragement, then go out and imitate that, as the Philippians imitated Paul.

Don't forget, however, that your aim is to imitate people who are Christ-like, not just people who you think are "cool." And as you begin to imitate them, be aware that others may be modeling themselves after you. How will your attitude rub off on them?

Reflection

Why is attitude so important to a leader's ability to effectively lead?

Attitude rubs off. With a bad attitude a leader will cause his/her people to fail, lose power, unity and hope.

What areas of your attitude do you need to work on? It might be a good idea for you to ask your parents and friends to help you answer this question.

Sometimes my attitude is bitter and unforgiving. ~~~~~~~~ I am a positive person but there are times especially when I stress out where my attitude goes from positive to negative

Are there certain times when you find it difficult to have a good attitude? Identify those times or situations, and list some ways that you can keep a more Christ-like attitude.

Sometimes it's hard to have a good attitude when everything seems to be going against you. We need to be thankful for all situations. ~~and it~~ and see the good in everything or moment.

The attitudes of others can quickly rub off on you. Describe how you've seen the attitudes of others affect you.

When my brother is being a "little punk" his bad attitude makes me angry and then my attitude reflects his.

One day, not long ago, a young man set out to make his home in a great city. As he approached his destination, he stumbled over an old man lying by the side of the road.

"What are the people like in this city?" asked the young man.

The old man replied, "What are they like where you came from?"

"Oh my—they are a terrible lot," reported the young man, "mean, untrustworthy, detestable in all respects."

"Ah," said the old man, "you will find them the same in the city ahead."

The young man hung his head and continued dejectedly toward the great city. Scarcely had he gone when another young traveler stumbled over the old man. He, too, stopped and inquired about the people in the city before him. Again the old man asked about the people in the place the traveler had just left.

"They were fine people. Honest, industrious and generous to a fault—I was sorry to leave," declared the second traveler.

Responded the wise one, "So you will find them in the city ahead."

Your expectations can alter your attitude, so beware of what you expect of people or situations.

List some expectations _desires._ that you have of people in your life. Do you feel that these expectations are hindering your attitude in any way?

> I want people to be happy, to see the good in all things. Sometimes this desire makes me angry because I don't understand the difficulty in being positive.

Attitude produces action. List some actions you would like to see in your leadership life and then consider what attitudes are needed to produce that result.

> I'd like to see many at my school being more positive, helping eachother, accepting, forgiving and respectful. To acheive this I would need to hold a positive attitude and display the attitude and actions I would like to see put in action. Be thankful, gracious, positive, helpful, respectful, patience and loyalty.

Empowerment

"What makes greatness is
starting something that lives after you." [1]
—Ralph Sockman

"The final test of a leader is that he leaves
behind him in other men the conviction and
will to carry on." [2]
—Walter Lippman

"And the things you have heard me
say in the presence of many witnesses entrust to
reliable men who will also be qualified to teach others."
—The Apostle Paul to a young leader
named Timothy in
2 Timothy 2:2

141

A LEADER

MEEKNESS INTEGRITY VISION ATTITUDE EMPOWER

CHRIST-LIKENESS

We can now add the fifth pillar of leadership to our structure. *Empowerment* is the pillar tied to your legacy of leadership. By empowering others to lead, you will ensure that the work that you started will continue beyond you.

I have a friend who, as a student, led a large campus ministry at a major university. The ministry organized meetings each Thursday night, packing in hundreds of college students anxious to hear the Word. As a result, my friend played a significant role on campus evangelizing, equipping, and encouraging many undergrads. When it came time for this friend to graduate, he was rewarded with a celebration party from those who had been under his leadership. He received gifts, thank you's, and testimonials of his influence. But when the next fall semester started, the meetings were discontinued.

Was this friend of mine a successful leader? He wielded great influence and he accomplished a lot, but did he *lead*? No, he did not. You are ultimately successful as a leader if the work that you are doing continues beyond you.

Our culture is replete with "personality cults"—organizations, churches, ministries, and events that have a charismatic figure-head. But a leader should not create a mini-dictatorship where he is the focus. Instead, you should be giving away leadership by training others to carry on after you are gone. As successful businessman Harvey Firestone said, "It is only as we develop others that we permanently succeed.[3]

Pass the ball

In many ways, coaching my son's youth soccer team taught me the importance of empowering others. At five years old, it was the first opportunity Bryan and his teammates had to play "organized" sports. Their lack of maturity and skill showed throughout the winless season. As a team, our biggest problem was that no one would pass the ball to a teammate. Once a player got the ball he would dribble down the field until swarmed by the other team. The teams that won were those that passed the ball to the open man. By being selfish and not allowing others to receive the soccer ball, we not only lost every game, we never scored a goal for the entire season! So it is with leadership. As a leader, you must constantly look for opportunities to pass the ball—to empower others to do what you are doing.

In *Pilgrim's Progress*, John Bunyan wrote, "My sword I give to him that shall succeed me in my pilgrimage, and my courage and skill to him that can get it. My marks and scars I carry with me, to be a witness for me, that I have fought His battles who now will be my rewarder."[4] To lead effectively you must constantly be passing the ball of leadership to others, empowering them to lead.

What is empowerment?

Empowerment is the act of endowing someone with the knowledge, tools, motivation and authority to continue the mission of the team.

143

An old mentor of mine, Tom Nelson, used to ask me, "Where are your men?" I knew exactly what he was getting at. Tom often reminded those he mentored that we needed to develop a group of people around us to receive the baton of leadership. Tom exemplified this principle in his own life; the church he pastors is led by servant leaders he nurtured, and he still seeks to empower leaders in his church.

Jesus empowered His men to do what He had been doing. He passed the baton by saying, "As the Father has sent Me, I also send you" (John 20:21). Jesus knew that His time on earth in human form was limited and that He had to prepare His men to continue what He had begun. As servant leaders, we too must continually give away our leadership to others.

Through the years, millions have learned about God's desire for a relationship with them thanks to the Billy Graham Crusades. The crusade team has been the same for decades: Cliff Burrows as emcee, George Beverly Shay as worship leader, and Billy Graham preaching. However, these three saints are nearing the end of their days, and they know it. They also know that, for the ministry to continue, they must empower others to take leadership. In watching a Crusade on television, you will notice that others are now more visible than in the past. Graham and his friends understand that their leadership legacy will be measured by how well they give their mission away.

The good and the bad of empowerment

Two things can happen when you pass the ball; one is good and one is bad. But if you haven't truly committed to giving leadership away, they will both be bad.

It's possible that those you sought to empower to continue the mission will lead poorly—a bad result. But far more dangerous is the pitfall that accompanies the good result.

The good result of empowerment happens when those we give

leadership to follow with competence and success—when they take the mantle of influence and serve faithfully.

The danger comes from our old nature. Here is the potential "bad" of empowerment. Seeing our work furthered by faithful men is viewed as a threat by our prideful, selfish old natures. What if those I empower lead better than I did? Could it be that I am not irreplaceable? Is it possible that I could one day be succeeded by a new and improved model?

Many leaders who feel this threat seek to appease their pride by faking a commitment to empowerment—relying instead on what I call "ghost empowerment." In this scenario, a leader "gives away" his leadership only to take it back when things are not done his way. This form of leadership is more destructive than never giving it away in the first place. Imagine the tension you would experience if, after being given responsibility and authority, it was taken away by the one who gave it to you—and during the most difficult times of the mission! A soccer game is never won if teammates fight for possession of the ball.

Allow setbacks

"Force may subdue, but Love gains; and he that forgives first, wins the laurel."[5]   —William Penn

When you turn over responsibility to others, you must allow them the freedom to fail. There will always be the possibility that the one you empower fails miserably. Empower anyway.

As a servant leader, you know that freedom fosters creativity, diligence, and loyalty. By allowing setbacks, you create trust in your team, inspiring those you lead to earn that trust. It is true that there is a danger that your trust will be abused, but it is far less dangerous than the alternative—the certainty that your followers will never learn bold leadership.

Thomas Edison had the crazy idea that he could foil the dark with a glass bulb that radiated light. After making preparations to assemble this technical marvel, he formed a team of men for the tedious job. It took the team 24 continuous hours to construct the first light bulb. Once the job was finished, the bulb was given to a young helper to carry upstairs to another laboratory. Nervously and cautiously the boy cradled the bulb in his hands as he mounted the stairs. When he reached the top stair, the unthinkable happened; he dropped the bulb and it shattered!

Edison's response was brilliant. The team immediately went to work for another 24 hours, and when the exhausted group finished, Edison took the bulb and handed it to the same boy to carry up the stairs.[6]

You should understand that those you serve through leadership will be successful to the degree you have trained them and given them freedom. By their success you will be able to judge your success as a leader. Plutarch was right when he wrote, "From their errors and mistakes the wise and good learn wisdom for the future."[7]

Challenge others to lead

Stepping out of the crowd and into leadership is a scary proposition for many. Those that you empower may be reticent about striking out on their own. But it is important to remember that nothing significant was ever accomplished without someone first taking a significant risk.

Dave Simmons was a good friend of mine before his tragic death. He would meet with me and a handful of other men every Tuesday morning to challenge, encourage, and teach us about being leaders. Throughout our three years together he would constantly remind us that soon we would need to start a small group of our own to teach what we had learned to others. Each time he reminded us of our impending separation, I felt anxious and scared. But when the Tuesday morning came when he told us we were ready to leave the nest and begin our own small group, I remember still feeling anxious but also feeling prepared and competent thanks to Dave's careful training and empowering.

Encourage

The word encourage literally means to "call to one's side." To encourage someone you lead is to stand by his side in thick and thin, to strengthen, and to commend. Tom Peters, business leadership guru, believes in generously doling out credit. He says, "Some people are real misers. They act as if giving others credit will somehow diminish themselves. What rot! Put simply... giving credit costs you nothing, and nets you big-time."[8] Sending "thank you" notes, giving gifts, showering people with "embarrassing" praise in front of their peers, adding their name to a project, etc., will give your team a sense of accomplishment like nothing else will. J.C. Staehle, after analyzing many surveys, found that the principal causes of unrest among workers are things that good encouragers can avoid. The number one reason for unrest on a team is failure to give credit for ideas, achievements, or creativity.

Retired U.S. Army Major General Aubrey "Red" Newman says in his book on leadership, "In command and leadership many qualities, attributes and techniques are required – including drive, force, judgment, perception, and others. But nothing can replace the inspiration and lift that comes from commending a job well done."[9] Take every opportunity as a leader to encourage those that you serve.

Share

"Share" may be the first word you remember your mother saying to you. My good friend Joe White, president of Kanakuk Kamps in Branson, Missouri, knows the value of sharing or "giving it away" and has taught this principle to others throughout his life of leadership. He has always been more than willing to share "trade secrets" with others in the camping industry. Without fear of being overtaken by his competition, Joe helps others to achieve excellence in their own camps. He understands the truth that most learn in kindergarten and forget by adulthood: the importance of sharing. In fact, Joe practices sharing to an embarrassing extent. I often saw him take off his shirt and give it to someone who said they liked it. The recipient always tried to refuse it, but Joe would insist, saying he had a lot of shirts he could wear. We were always careful not to compliment him on his shorts!

As a servant leader, you should strive to give away everything you have, knowing that everything has been given to you as a gift. As Peter Marshall said so well, "The measure of life is not its duration, but its donation."[10]

Each one of us, deep down inside, hopes that when we leave a group, church, school, or club, it will collapse because we aren't there. And we are a little surprised and disappointed if it doesn't. It's the nature of man to be self-centered. But as Christians seeking to become Christ-like, we must decide that our part on the team is to prepare others to lead and when they do, we should cheer them on.

What you know now. . .

- Empowerment is passing the ball of leadership.
- The right perspective makes empowerment a win/win situation.
- Give people the freedom to fail.
- Challenge others to lead.
- Encourage those you challenge.
- Share.

CHAPTER EIGHT

Study Section

When Tom Landry died, the football world lost a great leader. After his death, Landry was remembered for his stoic demeanor and his superb character.

Lee Roy Jordan was a star linebacker for the Dallas Cowboys under Landry's tutelage from 1963-76. After Landry passed away, Jordan remembered his old coach as someone who was "so stable, so consistent. He never got excited," Jordan said. "He never got down. He didn't show great emotions when things were going right and he didn't show great emotions when things were going wrong. I think that made him a great leader."

Landry's passion for the Lord and his spiritual consistency fueled his leadership ability. People knew where he stood in his faith and he consistently practiced his preach. This enabled him to not only help produce great football players like Jordan and Roger Staubach, but he also empowered some of his players to go out and become great coaches.

When Dan Reeves played for Landry, he studied him closely. After his playing career ended, Reeves became an assistant coach to the Cowboys. This gave him a little more time to observe the man whom he so admired.

"[Landry] was someone who had tremendous knowledge of the NFL," Reeves later commented. "He had a strong Christian faith that was unusual at that time. And he didn't just talk it. He walked it too."[11]

When Reeves moved on to become a head NFL coach, he tried to pattern himself after Landry. The lessons he learned from his former coach and mentor empowered Reeves to become a championship coach who led both Denver and later Atlanta to the Super Bowl. Landry not only empowered Reeves to leadership success, but also scores of other coaches, players, and associates were challenged by his empowering life.

Your willingness to lead coupled with your consistency in faith will give you the ability to empower others to become leaders. When people respect you, they will watch you and study the choices and decisions that you make. Your leadership will empower others to become great leaders. Who is watching you today?

A Message from the Word

For we know, brothers loved by God, that he has chosen you, because our gospel came to you not simply with words, but also with power, with the Holy Spirit and with deep conviction. You know how we lived among you for your sake. You became imitators of us and of the Lord; in spite of severe suffering, you welcomed the message with the joy given by the Holy Spirit. And so you became a model to all believers in Macedonia and Achaia—your faith in God has become known everywhere. Therefore we do not need to say anything about it, for they themselves report what kind of reception you gave us.

1 Thessalonians 1:4-9a

In his book, *Disciples Are Made Not Born,* Walter A. Henrichsen discusses the importance and effects of discipling another person. Henrichsen writes:

Jesus had world vision. He expected His men to have world vision. Jesus expected them to see the world through the disciples that they would produce, just as He had seen the world through the 12 men He had raised up. . . . When Jesus saw Peter, He did not see him as he was but as he would someday be. There is tremendous potential in the life of one man.[12]

In the Message from the Word, we looked at yet another passage

150

written by Paul. What an example of empowerment! Paul constantly encouraged his disciples to model themselves after him. He brought up new leaders, like Timothy and Luke, and empowered them to also go out and proclaim the gospel.

Paul learned how to do this from the ultimate example of empowerment, the Lord Jesus Christ. Jesus knew the importance of sending out disciples to teach and empower others to lead the world into reconciliation with the Father. Paul took this knowledge and applied it to those that he met along his missionary journeys.

Your life as a servant leader depends upon your ability to empower those that you influence. Are you teaching others to become great leaders?

Reflection

Why do you think it's so important for leaders, especially servant leaders, to help build and strengthen new leaders?

To spread the "positive" power in an amazing amount. So it multiplied and thrives.

multiplication of leaders = multiplication of followers.

Has someone effectively empowered you in your life? How did they do it?

A youth pastor before I came to a Christian school. empowered me to talk to the unbelievers of my public school.

Why do you think Jesus empowered only 12 men instead of doing more "big events"?

With only 12 men, Jesus could impact a few in a major way as opposed to impacting many in a minor way.

Before the disciples could successfully lead and train others, they spent an estimated three years in Jesus' presence. They soaked up all the information and wisdom that they could from the Lord. Are you doing that? Why do you think knowledge and wisdom are so important? And what are the differences between the two?

I am not sponging as I should. Wisdom is the application of knowledge.

In the world of sports, there are two categories that competitors fall into—individual sports or team sports. I would like to assert the belief that there is, actually, no such thing as an "individual sport." There are sports where a single individual competes against other individuals, but no one got there individually. In fact, these people often have a team of people around them at all times.

Shannon Miller, a two-time Olympian and the most decorated gymnast of all time, knows a little bit about how many people it takes to reach the top. Although gymnastics is technically an individual sport, gymnasts do not get to that level on their own. First, there is the coach. Steve Nuno coached Shannon from the time she was a child all the way through her Olympic career. But he wasn't the only one who worked with Shannon to get her through training. She needed a choreographer to put together her routines, a masseuse to loosen up her tight muscles, a doctor and trainer to make sure she didn't get hurt, parents to pay the bills, and multiple others to challenge and encourage her.

This holds true for any athlete. No one could get anywhere all on their own! Where would they find the motivation and the instruction? We were not meant to accomplish things on our own. God designed us to be creatures in need of encouragement and help. As a leader, you are in a phenomenal position to help build other leaders and you will be amazed at the growth you experience in the process!

Where are the men and women that you will empower? Do you know someone who could use your empowerment? It is probably already someone who looks up to you and considers you as a role model (a younger sibling, a junior member of the team, an underclassman, a new person at work, etc.). Make a list of these people and consider how you can empower them.

Brianne (my sister): get her to Church
Aaron (my brother): same.
Marty: go with him to seminars
        or meetings at College.
        (or just encourage him to).
Annie: get her to Church.
Chris: encourage him to use
        his musical abilities for
        worship.

Roadblocks To Leadership

*"The very difficulty
of a problem evokes abilities or
talents which would otherwise, in happy
times, never emerge to shine."
—Horace [1]*

I t would be foolish to assume, now that you understand the five pillars of leadership, that your influence will go untested and unchallenged. As you begin to apply these leadership principles, it is wise to realize that the world is not anxiously awaiting your coronation as leader. On the contrary, there exists a culture that is adverse to leadership, inherently selfish, and overtly rebellious. Throughout history there have always been more incentives not to be a leader than to pursue influence.

The great task now is to recognize, understand, and overcome the roadblocks to leadership. Adversity in leadership is inevitable. The wise leader accepts this and views obstacles as the very things that will create strength and endurance. An acorn planted on the forest floor and one planted on a barren hill will have divergent growth cycles. The tree growing under the protection of the forest canopy will emerge spindly and weak with shallow roots, but the hilltop oak will grow thick and strong. This oak anchors itself with a root system stretching in all directions, digging deep into the earth. It does so, by necessity, to brace itself against nature's forces. Adversity makes one tree strong, and the lack of adversity makes the other weak.

Seeing spots.

What do you see?

156

Most people would say a "spot," "dot," "hole," or "circle." Yes, but look again. This time you may observe that it is a *black* spot. And on further review, you notice it is perfectly round. All true, but there is more. The perfectly round, black spot is on a white field. It is on a page in a book in your hands in a room. Check your peripheral vision and see around the spot. Now you are aware of much more.

The spot is representative of the roadblocks to leadership in our lives—those reasons why you might not want to lead. And everything around the spot is comparable to the opportunities we tend to miss in leadership. Many opportunities are missed because of where our focus lies.

Let's list those obstacles that we perceive as being in the way of leadership. It's as easy as filling in the blank because most road-blocks fall into these three categories:

Fear of ____risk____ (failure, embarrassment, people, the unknown, mistakes, risk)

Lack of ___opportunity___ (abilities, talent, resources, charisma, opportunity)

Tendency to be ___faithless___ (lazy, selfish, overly critical, bossy, unorganized, faithless)

Fear

Undoubtedly, the most imposing of all obstacles is fear. The fear of failure, rejection, loss, embarrassment, and pain are formidable foes in your leadership quest. But they are also vulnerable to the (not-so-secret weapon) of the Christian: faith. Having fear is telling God that you are doubtful that He can take care of His assignment—that the plans He has revealed are in jeopardy. It is abandoning trust in what is true to embrace the "what if's" of the unknown.

Oswald Chambers rightly said, "The remarkable thing about fearing God is that when you fear God, you fear nothing else. Whereas if you do not fear God, you fear everything else."[2] Fear is inevitable. You will fear. The question is "whom or what will you fear?"

In the diagram below (figure #6), you can see the decision/consequence progression that we all experience. All of us begin with the same reality. How you respond to that reality determines your fear.

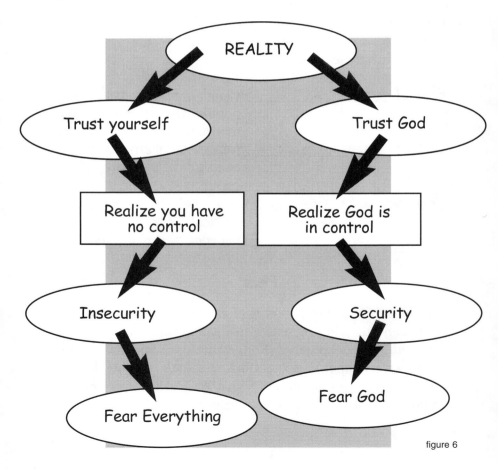

figure 6

In Ecclesiastes we learn of King Solomon's pursuit of fulfill-ment. He was rich enough, powerful enough, smart enough and famous enough to partake of everything the world had to offer. All this to ascertain if joy and peace might be found outside of a relationship with God. By the end of the book, Solomon has seen it, done that, and been there and comes to the realization that when one distills life to its essence, few things matter outside of our fear of God. He says in Ecclesiastes 12:13, "Now all has been heard; here is the conclusion of the matter: Fear God and keep His commandments, for this is the whole duty of man."

The wisest course of action is to first trust God as the *reality* of reality hits. After that, everything else takes care of itself.

The "biggy"—fear of failure

All men differ, but there is one thing that seems to be common to us all and that is fear of failure. The strong emotions attached to this fear are sometimes overwhelming. Shame, embarrassment, rejection, and guilt can make a person weak at the mere sugges-tion of the possibility. But to trust God in the reality of your circumstances provides the opportunity to overcome these deceiving emotions with confidence.

I remember hearing Dr. James Dobson relate a highly personal experience on the radio. Dr. Dobson had been invited to appear on the Phil Donahue Show. At the time, the program was the top-rated daytime talk show on the air. The producers of the program had invited Dobson and a non-Christian psychologist to share their views about spanking and corporal punishment. Just before it was time to begin taping, Donahue came out into the studio to warm up the audience. He asked the audience if any of them believed a parent should never spank their child. Not one hand was raised. Donahue persisted, "You mean to tell me that there is not one person in this audience that believes spanking is a form of child abuse?" Several hands sheepishly went up. Obviously pleased, Donahue took his place to begin taping the show.

Throughout the entire program, Donahue only went to those few people to take questions. Halfway through the taping Dr. Dobson realized he had walked into an ambush. When the smoke had cleared and he was back in his hotel room, Dr. Dobson related how he stared out the window and cried out to God. "Why did You embarrass me like that? I came here on Your business and You allowed me to be made a fool of on national television." He then recalled the truth that came to him in that moment: God never promised us that we would look good, be respected, or be considered credible when we step out for Him. We should be faithful to His work even at the risk of rejection, ridicule, and embarrassment. As I heard this story, I was reminded of Job's affirmation of faith in the character of God. In Job 13:15, as Job is tormented by tragic circumstances, he avows, "Though He slay me, will I hope in Him." Failure is a part of growth, and how you deal with it will determine the extent of your growth as a leader.

Lack

Another roadblock to leadership is the individual's perception that he lacks the personality, confidence, character qualities, resources, support, reputation, or ability that is needed to succeed as a leader. We all can look around us and see others that are more gifted and talented than we are. That we are not Superman is hardly a news flash.

To fret over the lack of something is once again saying something about who you believe God to be. Is He not able to fill in the gaps in your leadership? Can He not provide what you need to be an effective influencer?

Moses was well aware of his lack when he was called by God to lead the Hebrew nation out of Egypt. He pleaded with God not to send him because he lacked some of the necessary traits to lead. Then God taught us all when He reminded Moses that he was not alone, but God Himself would be directing his leadership. Like Moses, we become keenly aware of our lack when we assume that we are in control and responsible for the results. And like Moses, we must understand the nature of God resting in the assurance that He is in control.

Our lack is not a weakness but rather a strength. God tells us in 2 Corinthians 12:9 that His strength is made perfect in our weakness. Our need is the vacuum God desires to fill.

Every Wednesday afternoon at a Worldview Academy Leadership Camp we take a street evangelism trip to a college campus. The students, as well as myself, are keenly aware that we lack certain abilities if we expect to successfully share the good news of God's love. The thought of witnessing to a college student petrifies most, if not all, of our teenage students. How can they possibly be effective in presenting the gospel? Lack is as evident as a death mask on each face. The outbound bus ride is always the same: silence, fear, and anguished prayer. And the return trip is invariably the same: rejoicing, laughter, and relief. The students learn in a practical way that where we lack, God fills in the blanks. The debrief afterward is always a sweet time of relating how God provided the right words at the right time and of how His strength was perfected in our weakness.

Tendency

Every team knows its own weaknesses but strives to conceal them from the enemy while working to develop strength in that area. When a sports team is scouting an opponent, the coaches will chart the other team's plays to determine if there is some obvious tendency to call certain plays in certain situations. Do they tend to run to the wide side of the field, drive to the basket with their dominant hand, or hit to the opposite field? By discovering tendencies in an opponent, a great advantage can be gained.

I remember playing against a running back with incredible

talent. He had single-handedly shredded the defenses of several other teams. But in watching the game films, we noticed that when the running back was going to carry the ball he would put his mouthpiece in. Otherwise he would let his mouthpiece dangle from his facemask before the ball was snapped. This seemingly insignificant tip allowed our players to shut down this athlete and inhibit his team's chances of scoring.

This applies to you. You have weaknesses in your personality, character, and attitudes. We all do. The chore is to work on the weakness without allowing the enemy to exploit it.

Satan seeks to use those areas of our life that are less developed to defeat us as leaders. He cannot read our minds, but he has a scouting report on our actions, and he is a great predictor of human nature. What are those tendencies in your life that can be used against you—laziness, apathy, jealousy, prejudice, lust, or bitterness? I imagine one of these is a gap in your armor and that the enemy is aware and is attempting to utilize this tendency against you. The best way to deal with a fatal tendency is to confront it earnestly, asking God to heal, change, or redirect the flaw. This takes time, effort, and honesty with God. But unless it is faced, this tendency will compromise your ability to succeed as a leader.

The sum of all fears

Fear, tendency, and lack are all first cousins in that they spring from the same unbiblical assumption—that God is not capable or willing to fulfill His plan. When we add up all the reasons that we cannot succeed in leadership, we find the sum to be distrust in God's power, plan, and provision. Trust is our weapon to battle fear, tendency and lack.

I loathe flying. There is not enough Dramamine in the world to take the edge off of my stomach when I'm in an airplane. The reason I dislike it so passionately is that I am not in control, and I don't trust the pilot. I especially dislike landing. During the entire final approach, I am gripping the armrests, pushing imaginary pedals with my feet, and leaning from side to side in an attempt to level out the plane for a smooth landing. The pilot needs this extra assistance because, in my mind, he probably got his license at Wal-Mart. I don't trust him or her or whoever is steering this flying machine. I have data to support this belief. In a recent Gallup Poll, people were asked to rank which professions they trusted most and the top ten were:

1. Pharmacist – 68%
2. Clergy – 59%
3. Doctor – 56%
4. College Teacher - 55%
5. Dentist - 54%
6. Policeman – 49%
7. Engineer – 49%
8. Funeral Director – 36%
9. Banker – 34%
10. Journalist – 23%

Do you see airline pilot anywhere on the list? Neither do I! So I am justified, right? Everyone around me seems oblivious to the grave danger that we are in, yet I sweat on. They are calm, and I'm as nervous as a calf in a squeeze shoot. Why? Because they trust—and I don't.

As much as we'd like to think we are, we are never in control. I don't like the saying "Let go and let God" because it supposes that we have no personal responsibility. But there is a smidgen of truth in it. He is in control, and we must trust. God is not our co-pilot and we are not His. We must remain seated in the passenger section with our seatbelt fastened, tray table and seatback in their full, upright and locked position. We may want to wrest the control stick away from Him but, as in landing a plane, that is suicide. Allow Him to work and direct His plan while trusting Him.

What you know now...

- Roadblocks are not as big as they appear.
- All roadblocks to leadership can be filed into three categories: fear, lack, and tendency.
- Distrust is the sum of all fears.
- Trust is the silver bullet that defeats all roadblocks.

C H A P T E R   N I N E
Study Section

When Andy was little, everyone thought he was just really shy. He hated school and cried every morning before the bus came. When he got older, he still cried, but in private because they told him he was "too old for tears." Andy's parents urged him to get out and meet people. They bribed him in order to get him to go to school dances and functions. He always went but hid in a corner, avoiding all eye contact. He knew they were all staring at him. In fact, everyone stared at him wherever he went.

When it came time to go to college, Andy chose a small community college close to home so he could still live with his parents. On the first day of school, Andy went to the park instead of his classes because he knew that the professor would make them go around the room and introduce themselves. The thought of speaking in front of people made him sick to his stomach. But day two was even worse. Andy's professors would pick people out of the classroom to read, or to answer a question, and twice Andy was called upon. Mortified, he went home and told his parents he was dropping out.

Andy suffers from a common problem known as social phobia or social anxiety. People who struggle with this particular phobia truly believe that wherever they go they are being watched and judged. If left untreated, social anxiety can cause a person to completely withdraw from life. They are paralyzed by their fear, and they live in mental torment.

Social phobia boils down to nothing more than intense fear that shackles its victims. This fear has the power to cause health problems such as ulcers, muscle spasms and fatigue. It affects 15 million Americans in any given year, yet no one seems to really understand it.

Do you suffer from "social leadership anxiety?" Do you fear the idea of leading others? Well, one thing you should understand is that fear is inevitable. It's what you do with your fear that matters. Are you succumbing to your fears, or are you facing and replacing your fears with the fear of God?

A Message from the Word

Do not call conspiracy everything that these people call conspiracy; do not fear what they fear, and do not dread it. The Lord Almighty is the one you are to regard as holy, He is the one you are to fear, He is the one you are to dread, and He will be a sanctuary. . . I will wait for the Lord, who is hiding His face from the house of Jacob. I will put my trust in Him.

Isaiah 8:12-14a; 17

The world presents plenty of things to fear these days. As the free world fights a war against terrorism, a seemingly unbeatable foe, it desperately needs courageous leadership. It is not the time to "fear what they fear." We should abandon our fears and replace them with the power of God.

Throughout the book of Exodus, we are able to read the specific instructions that God gave Moses and the Israelites for the building of the Ark of the Covenant. The tent in which the precious mercy seat would be harbored was accessible only to the high priest. From the description we are given, the Holy of Holies was magnificent. It was created out of the finest materials and stones. This was God's means of communicating to His children. When the high priest entered the Holy of Holies, he was most likely overcome with an overwhelming sense of God's presence. He could not stand in that room. He would fall to his knees in fear and awe as he looked to the mercy seat and the two large cherubim that flanked it. This became God's sanctuary, and it was here that He communicated with His chosen ones.

Often, we as Christians make God out to be somewhat of a

"cosmic pushover." We don't see Him as the Ruler and Judge that He is. God deserves the utmost respect and fear that we can give Him. This type of fear is a healthy fear. Unlike the fear that accompanies social anxiety, the fear of God actually strengthens us instead of rendering us powerless.

In times of uncertainty, fear God, not man, because God's power is much mightier than man's power. Look to Him as your sanctuary. When God sent Jesus to die for our sins, He suddenly made the Holy of Holies accessible to everyone. We are all given the chance to enter His presence and sit at His throne. And when we do that, our God meets us where we are. Fear Him and enter into His sanctuary—it is there, and only there, that you will find His peace and power.

Reflection

What is the greatest fear you have in taking on leadership?

reaching out, speaking up, total failure, and rejection of from listeners, or listeners not exactly listening. Mainly it is my fear of failure.

Why is that fear NOT beyond the power of God to overcome?

It isn't. All it is, is my own selfish thought that I won't impress or affect people. God can and will overcome this fear.

What tendencies of weakness or strengths do you see in your own character? How can you work on those in order that Satan doesn't turn them against you?

Sometimes I feel affected by opinions of other people.

What does the fear of God mean to you? Do you see Him as your sanctuary?

The fear of God to me is the great extent of his power. Fear Him with respect, love, awe, his realness.

Rosa Parks, mother of the Civil Rights Movement, was arrested in 1955 for refusing to give up her seat on a bus to a white man. Boycotts and protests followed, and eventually the Supreme Court ruled racial segregation unconstitutional. In her book, *Quiet Strength*, she wrote:

I have learned over the years that knowing what must be done does away with fear. When I sat down on the bus that day, I had no idea history was being made—I was only thinking of getting home. But I had made up my mind. After so many years of being a victim of the mistreatment my people suffered, not giving up my seat—and whatever I had to face afterwards-was not important. I did not feel any fear sitting there. I felt the Lord would give me the strength to endure whatever I had to face. It was time for someone to stand up—or in my case, sit down. So I refused to move.[3]

When you look beyond the circumstances around you and you do not give in to the pressure of fear, you can accomplish great things. When Rosa Parks sat down, she wasn't planning on changing the course of history—her feet hurt, that's all. As she was pressured by the irrational and unfair rules of the time, she did not give into her fear but trusted in what was right. When fear sets in, you have two options: tremble or trust. What will you do?

Look up and read the following verses: Proverbs 29:25; Exodus 18:21; Deuteronomy 10:20; Psalms 19:9a. In what ways in the past has God proven that HE can handle any situation or fear that you may be struggling with today? In what ways have you witnessed others handle fear successfully?

Prov. 29:25 The fear of man brings a snare but → who trusts in the Lord will be exalted.

Exod: 18:21 select men who fear God, honest → place them as leaders.

Deut: 10:20 you shall fear the Lord, your God: you shall serve him and cling to Him + swear by his name.

Psalms 19:9a. the fear of the Lord is clean, enduring forever.

At diabetes camp the little kids are still afraid of taking injections but as they get older they do what they have to do. this is like how we need to do what God has planned for us. I'm sure he didn't intend for most to be lazy bums. I need to get over my fears by prayer to him and persistance and do what God wants me to do.

Whatever It Takes

"Screw your courage to the sticking place."

– William Shakespeare[1]

Now you know the core principles in preparing for leadership and the roadblocks that threaten that leadership—but knowing them is not enough. You must now decide that you will do the hard work that is ahead, apply the five pillars to your life, and persevere when difficult days come. You must commit to do whatever it takes.

Mike Singletary was an All-Pro linebacker for the Chicago Bears and considered by many to be one of the greatest players in the history of the NFL. When he was developing his skills as a linebacker for the Baylor Bears, he used to write "whatever it takes" on the tape around his wrists. He was committed to doing just that, within the rules, to attain excellence. It was this attitude that allowed him to overcome his small size to play a "big man's" game. He did whatever it took to be a champion not only on the field, but also in the weight room, off-season, in class, and in his personal life. This is the attitude that you must have as a servant leader, doing whatever it takes to attain Christ-likeness in your life and leadership.

In doing whatever it takes, there are three things you need to remember as you wade into the currents of leadership.

Be steadfast

Shadrach, Meshach and Abednego chose to follow God instead of bowing down to the idols of man. They were threatened and then sentenced to die by incineration in the royal furnace. "Make the fire hotter—hotter—seven times hotter!" Nebuchadnezzer yelled. The fire was so hot that the guards holding the prisoners could not bear it and were burned to death. In the face of this torment, the last words (or so Nebuchadnezzer thought!) uttered by Shadrach, Meshach, and Abednego were steadfast indeed.

"Our God whom we serve is able to deliver us from the furnace of blazing fire; and He will deliver us out of your hand, O king. But even if He does not, let it be known to you, O king, that we are not going to serve your gods or worship the golden image that you have set up" (Daniel 3:17-18, NASV). These three men were steadfast in their commitment to doing whatever it took to remain excellent and obedient.

To be steadfast is to stay on your horse even when the bullets are whistling past and the bombs are exploding around you. Standing your ground can be dangerous, but the rewards are tremendous. Patriot Thomas Paine described the reward this way:

> "These are the times that try men's souls. The summer soldier and the sunshine patriot will, in this crisis, shrink from the service of their country; but he that stands it now, deserves the love and thanks of man and woman. Tyranny, like hell, is not easily conquered; yet we have this consolation with us, that the harder the conflict, the more glorious the triumph. What we obtain too cheap, we esteem too lightly: 'tis dearness only that gives every thing its value. Heaven knows how to put a proper price upon its goods; and it would be strange indeed, if so celestial an article as freedom should not be highly rated...I love the man that can smile in trouble, that can gather strength from distress, and grow brave by reflection. 'Tis the business of little minds to shrink; but he whose heart is firm, and whose conscience approves his conduct, will pursue his principles unto death."[2]

Steadfastness is sticking to what you believe and to your vision even in the face of opposition and realizing that the reward is to be valued above the praise of feeble men.

Be confident

God is in control. Period. Nothing that happens to you catches God by surprise. He is even in charge of making sure that your labor to become Christ-like is not in vain. Paul tells us in Philippians 1:6 that he is sure of God's plan for our lives: "For I am confident of this very thing, that He who began a good work in you will perfect it until the day of Christ Jesus."

On February 24, 1791, six days before his death at age 88, John Wesley wrote his last letter to William Wilberforce, a Member of Parliament, who was committed to the abolition of slavery and the slave trade. The battle over slavery continued for years, but in 1833, thanks largely to the efforts of Wilberforce, Parliament ratified the Emancipation Act outlawing slavery in England. The text of the letter follows. The "tract" to which Wesley refers was written by a former slave, Gustavus Vassa, who was born in 1745 in Africa, kidnapped, and sold as a slave in Barbados. In 1757 he was sent to England and was converted to Christianity.

Dear Sir:

Unless the divine power has raised you up to be as "Athanasius against the world," I see not how you can go through your glorious enterprise in opposing that execrable villainy, which is the scandal of religion, of England, and of human nature. Unless God has raised you up for this very thing, you will be worn out by the opposition of God and devils. But if God be for you, who can be against you? Are all of them stronger than God? O be not weary of well doing! Go on, in the name of God in the power of His might, till even American slavery (the vilest that ever saw the sun) shall vanish away before it.

Reading this morning a tract wrote by a poor African, I was particularly struck by the circum-

stance, that a man who has black skin, being wronged or outraged by a white man, can have no redress; it being a LAW in our Colonies that the OATH of a black man against a white goes for nothing. What villainy is this!

That He who has guided you from youth up may continue to strengthen you in this and all things is the prayer of, dear sir,
Your affectionate servant,
John Wesley

John Wesley was confident of what was unseen and unimaginable at the time, the abolition of slavery. Although the odds were against himself and Wilberforce, he knew that, God can accomplish anything. They were both confident that no matter what happened, they would be counted with those who loved others as they loved themselves. And their confidence paid off.

Confidence is not arrogance. Being arrogant about the Lord's work in your life is as ridiculous as a piece of coal being prideful about becoming a diamond. The coal was not responsible for anything—the work was done by the outside force that shaped it. Likewise, we should humbly rest in God and trust Him to mold us into the servant leader He desires.

Be focused

Keep your eyes on the goal of becoming a servant leader. If you do not, your path will be longer, harder, and more frustrating. Anyone seeking a goal wants the straightest, shortest route—and there is nothing wrong with desiring this as long as you avoid unbiblical shortcuts. But taking the shortest route requires focus.

I've always wanted to be a farmer, working the land and seeing a tangible result from my labors. I suppose that's why I love to talk about farming with farmers. I remember asking one farmer how he made the rows so straight in his fields. He cocked his cap and looked at me as if I had just asked him what ice was made of (I thought it was a pretty intelligent question coming from a non-farmer.) He said that all you need to do is pick out a point on the horizon across the field and keep heading for it. He added that to look to the side, back, or down will ruin your straight line and cause problems later.

So it is with our desire to be a leader. We must set our sights on the One who will make us that leader and start plowing. Looking to the sides or backwards at the distractions around us will only cause crookedness in our leadership.

Another important reason to remain focused in the process of becoming a leader is that error increases with distance. Take a look at the two arrows below (figure 7). You can see that the arrows are closest at point A. As the arrows project outward from that point, they distance themselves from each other.

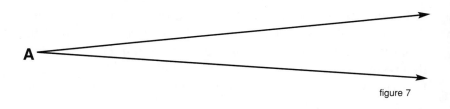

figure 7

If you begin to veer off the path, the longer you wait the more you will distance yourself from God's plan.

In C.S. Lewis' *Voyage of the Dawn Treader*, the cast of characters are on a journey to Aslan's country. The trip has been marked by many dangers and adventures. As they near the end of the voyage, most of them lose heart and agree to turn back. But Reepicheep, an irrepressible mouse and noble servant of Prince Caspian, shames them with these brave words:

"My own plans are made. While I can, I sail east in the *Dawn Treader*. When she fails me, I paddle east in my coracle. When she sinks, I shall swim east with my four paws. And when I can swim no longer, if I have not reached Aslan's country, or shot over the edge of the world in some vast cataract, I shall sink with my nose to the sunrise...."[3]

This mouse was no Mickey; he had a steadfast, confident focus. In the same way remain focused on the goal of Christ-likeness.

Take the risk!

"If one is forever cautious, can one remain a human being?"[4]
– Aleksandr Solzhenitsyn

The challenge of becoming a servant leader is before you. Now you must decide to take the risk of actually becoming one. It may help you to recognize that this risk is unavoidable for the Christian—following Christ encompasses servant leadership. As French statesman Paul De Gondi said, "That which is necessary is never a risk."[5]

The real risk, of course, is avoiding God's purpose for your life.

I have full confidence in the fact (that's right, fact) that if you apply what you have learned, diligently seek to lead through serving, and pursue Christ-likeness, you will be a success in whatever venture God has for you. And remember that to take the risk is more than half the battle. Teddy Roosevelt said it best when he spoke these words:

> "Far better it is to dare mighty things, to win glorious triumphs, even though checkered by failure, than to take rank with those poor spirits who neither enjoy much nor suffer much, because they live in the gray twilight that knows not victory nor defeat."[6]

177

So it shall be done

And having taken the risk to become a servant leader you can be assured that the results God desires will be realized through you. For the Bible assures us in 1 Peter 5:10, "After you have suffered [to become a student leader] for a little while, the God of all grace, who called you to His eternal glory in Christ, will Himself perfect, confirm, strengthen, and establish you [as a student leader]."

What you know now...

- Be prepared to do whatever it takes (within the rules).
- Be steadfast in the midst of opposition.
- Be confident by knowing that God's plan will prevail.
- Be focused on the goal of being a Christ-like leader.
- Take the risk of becoming a leader.

CHAPTER TEN

Study Section

In the fall of 1943, the 111th Medical Battalion made history as they camped out in "Hitler's back yard." The young troops were the first American soldiers to land on the mainland of Hitler's German-held Festung Europa. Hundreds lost their lives as they landed on the open beach and were attacked from overhead by the Germans. The 111th Medical Battalion was there for one reason.—to secure the beach and hold it until reinforcements could come. They had no idea how long that would take.

After they completed their mission, Glenn C. Clift, one of the soldiers, wrote a letter describing their ordeal. In the letter, he had a friend write about his experience. This unnamed soldier is a hero. This is what he wrote:

You see it was like this. I came in with the third wave, just like the other boys. It was around four-thirty, not quite daylight. How it was, I was dug in on the beach and there was a lieutenant there beside me in the slit trench. The lieutenant noticed one of the assault boats had been hit by an enemy artillery shell. . . It was down. Some of the boys were on fire. The boat was facing me and I saw an arm waving for help from the floor of the boat.

The first thing that came to mind was that if that was me out there I would want someone to come after me.

I threw off my equipment and the soldiers on the beach started hollering at me not to go. I went around trying to get a couple of volunteers to go with me but machine gun fire was pretty hot right then and all the fellows ducked down in their slit trenches to get away from it.

I kept teasing them and one of the boys says "I'll go with you." Then another guy said he would go too. . . .

We ran down the beach with heavy gunfire on us. The

boat was about forty yards from the shore and was burning pretty bad now. We started to swim out there. We could hear the bullets hitting the water all around us. It was pretty close. One of the boys wanted to turn back but we kept teasing him to come.

We reached the boat... these other two boys hung onto the ramp and I climbed up in the boat. They were four in there. A major and three enlisted men. The fire was so hot by then my clothes started steaming... The major was dead. The other three were wounded in the legs. I didn't know where else.

... I decided that we would have to leave the major and told the boys if they could swim one of the wounded men to the shore I could bring the other two. While we were coming in there was still machine gun fire all around us.

We started first-aid as soon as we hit the beach. While we were doing this I heard an awful blast. The boat I was on, the gas tank had blown.[7]

When this unknown medical soldier saw fellow medics in peril, he knew he could not leave them there to die. Against the urgings of others, he raced toward the burning boat. He even managed to recruit some help along the way. This man understood "whatever it takes."

As a leader, you will be discouraged from leading. As you run toward the front lines, you will be told that it's too dangerous, just stay back and protect yourself, don't risk yourself for others. As a leader, you will come under fire from the opposition. As a leader, you will have the opportunity to let those things discourage you, or you can press on, recruiting help from others, and do whatever it takes. Be steadfast in your resolve. Be courageous. Do whatever it takes to be the leader you are meant to be.

A Message from the Word

Let us not become weary in doing good, for at the proper time we will reap a harvest if we do not give up.

Galatians 6:9

Leadership is not an easy responsibility. It will take perseverance, endurance and strong will. Sometimes leadership is even quite risky. You may lose friends or popularity or recognition, but one thing is for sure—if you stand strong, you will never lose the respect of others or the pleasure of the Father. Yesterday is gone, tomorrow is not here, but today can be captured. Now is the time for your leadership!

Where will leadership take you? You will probably not know at first. Billy Graham had no idea the impact he would have on the world when he started preaching-he just followed His call. What's His call on your life? You may not figure that out right away, but have an open mind and heart.

Bill Devlin lives in Philadelphia with his wife and five children. No big deal, right? Philly is a nice place—lots of history. While this is true, it's also true that if you live in Philadelphia, you'd better live on the "right" side of town. Bill and his family do not live in the ideal part of Philadelphia. What often shocks people even more is the fact that they chose to live where they did. Years ago, Bill felt called to work with the urban poor. He felt a passion for drug addicts and criminals, but he couldn't seem to reach the people that he most wanted to affect. So he and his wife decided to move into the part of town that was best known for shootings, drugs and crime.

Bill is the first to admit that this wasn't an easy decision. He had his children to think about and their safety. He argued with the Lord for a long time before succumbing to His calling. Once he moved into town and began his ministry, the hardships began almost immediately. The Devlins have been robbed numerous times, they have been shot at, they have heard screams outside their house, and many other horrors. Bill was stabbed repeatedly by a mugger right outside his home and miraculously survived. Yet they continue to press on. Despite these many hardships, the Devlins have witnessed the conversion of hundreds of drug addicts, drug dealers, AIDS victims, and murderers. They are known throughout the country for their phenomenal work in the projects. Bill travels around the world speaking, encouraging others to reach out to those that seem unreachable. Bill Devlin is a servant leader. His labor is not in vain and the Word of God has not returned void. Bill Devlin is only just beginning to see the fruits of his "whatever it takes" labors, and he's been working at this for almost twenty years.

Do not lose heart in your leadership. In God's good time your good labor will produce the good results. And a portion of that good result will be your emergence as a servant leader.

Reflection

In what ways in the past have you done "whatever it takes" to achieve a desired goal? What have been the results?

My diabetes has been my big goal. I read books and magazines, learned to count carbohydrates, effectively administer my insulin, went to seminars all so that I could take better care of myself.

What motivates you to be steadfast in your quest for leadership?

Outcomes. So many times my thoughts of a vision or quest are filled with..."just imagine how amazing that would be." the possible outcome is my motivation.

182

As you consider "whatever it takes," list some of the things that you think it will take for you to reach your full potential as a servant leader?

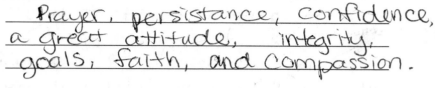

Prayer, persistance, confidence, a great attitude, integrity, goals, faith, and compassion.

On October 20, 1968, a few thousand spectators remained in the Mexico City Olympic Stadium awaiting the finish of the marathon. As the last few exhausted runners were carried off to first-aid stations, the spectators prepared to leave. As they began milling around, they heard the sounds of sirens and police whistles. Everyone stopped and turned toward the gates entering into the stadium. A lone figure, wearing the number 36 and the colors of Tanzania, limped into the stadium. His name was John Stephen Akhwari. During the race, Akhwari fell and badly injured his knee and ankle. With his battered leg bloody and bandaged, Akhwari grimaced with each step as he made his way around the 400-meter track. The spectators rose in excitement and cheered him on through his final steps. After crossing the finish line, Akhwari walked slowly off the field, the sound of applause still echoing the stadium. A reporter approached him and asked the question on everyone's mind: "Why did you continue the race after you were so badly injured?"

Akhwari politely replied, "My country did not send me 7,000 miles to start the race. They sent me 7,000 miles to finish it."

Run hard and finish strong—whatever it takes!

You have now studied in depth the role of a servant leader and the necessary components of successful leadership. Write down any thoughts or ideas that you have as you set out toward the role of a leader. Where will you start? What will change in your daily routine? Spend some time in prayer and ask the Lord to begin to prepare you for your role.

I'm going to start by. Changing my attitude, by acting as an example to all those who surround me. I'm going to stop running the Stop sign by my house and change my ways to keep/establish my integrity. I will be humble and compassionate for my friends and family and for helping them come closer to God. I'm going to get more "plugged" into my new church. Yeah! Oh! And eventually I would like to start my own small group when I feel I can get some people together.

TheBridge to Life

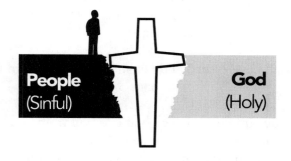

Beginning a relationship with Jesus Christ
©1997, The Navigators

Step One

God's Love and His Plan

God created us in His own image to be
His friend and to experience a full life assured of His
love, abundant and eternal.

Jesus said, "...I have come that they may have life,
and have it to the full." (John 10:10b)

"...we have peace with God through
our Lord Jesus Christ." (Romans 5:1)

Since God planned for us to have peace and
abundant life right now, why are most people not having
this experience?

Step Two

Our Problem: Separation from God

God created us in His own image to have abundant (meaning-ful) life. He did not make us robots to automatically love and obey Him, but He gave us a will and a freedom of choice. We chose to disobey God and to go our own willful way. We still make this choice today. This results in separation from God.

"For all have sinned and fall short of the glory of God." (Romans 3:23)

"...your iniquities have separated you from your God; your sins have hidden His face from you so that He will not hear." (Isaiah 59:2)

On our own, there's no way we can attain the perfection needed to bridge the gap to God. Through the ages, individuals have tried many ways...without success.

Good works won't do it...or religion... or money...or morality...or philosophy...

"There is a way that seems right to a man, but in the end it leads to death." (Proverbs 14:12)

Step Three

God's Remedy: The Cross

Jesus Christ is the only answer to this problem. He died on the cross and rose from the grave, paying the penalty for our sin and bridging the gap between God and people.

"For Christ died for sins one for all, the righteous for the unrighteous, to bring you to God..." (I Peter 3:18)

"For there is one God and one mediator between God and men, the man Jesus Christ." (I Timothy 2:5)

"But God demonstrates His own love for us in this: while we were still sinners, Christ died for us." (Romans 5:8)

Step Four

Our Response

Believing means trust and commitment—acknowledging our sinfulness, trusting Christ's forgiveness and letting Him control our life. Eternal, abundant life is a gift for us to receive.

"For God so loved the world that He gave His one and only Son, that whoever believes in Him shall not perish but have eternal life."
(John 3:16)

"I tell you the truth, whoever hears my word and believes Him who sent Me has eternal life and will not be condemned; he has crossed over from death to life." (John 5:24)

Is there any reason why you shouldn't cross over to God's side and be certain of eternal life?

How to receive Christ:

1. Admit your need (I am a sinner).
2. Be willing to turn from your sins (Repent).
3. Believe that Jesus Christ died for you on the cross and rose from the grave.
4. Through prayer, invite Jesus Christ to come in and control your life through the Holy Spirit (Receive Him as Lord and Savior of your life).

What to pray:

Dear Lord Jesus,
I know that I am a sinner and need Your forgiveness.
I believe that You died for my sins. I want to turn from my sins. I now invite you to come into my heart and life. I want to trust and follow You as the Lord and Savior of my life.

In Your name. Amen.

God's assurance of eternal life.

If you've prayed this prayer and trusted Christ, then the Bible says that you can be sure you have eternal life.

"...for, 'everyone who calls on the name of the
Lord will be saved.'" (Romans 10:13)

"For it is by grace you have been saved, through
faith—and this not from yourselves, it is the gift of God—
not by works, so that no one can boast." (Ephesians 2:8-9)

"He who has the Son has life;
he who does not have the Son of God does not have life.
I write these things to you who believe in the name of the
Son of God so that you may know that
you have eternal life." (I John 5:12-13)

Receiving Christ, we are born into God's family through the supernatural work of the Holy Spirit who indwells every believer...this is called regeneration or the "new birth."

Reprinted from The Bridge Illustration.
copyright NavPress. Used by permission of NavPress, Colorado Springs, CO. All rights reserved. For copies call (800) 366-7788 or www.navpress.com

Now what?

This is just the beginning of a wonderful new life in Christ. To deepen this relationship you should:

Spend Time with God. Your relationship with God, just like any other relationship, is strengthened by time spent together and communication. Maintain regular intake of the Bible to know Christ better. Talk to God in prayer every day.

Spend Time with Other Christians. You will be encouraged in your new relationship with God by hanging out with other people who want to love God and serve others. Tell others about your new faith in Christ.

Worship, fellowship and serve with other Christians in a church where Christ is preached.

As Christ's representative in a needy world, demonstrate your new life by your love and concern for others.

If you still have questions about becoming a Christian or just who God is, please feel free to call Worldview Academy at 830-620-5203. There is someone there who would love to talk with you more about this important decision.

If you are now part of God's family as a new Christian, you can finish *The Greatest Among You.* You may want to read this along with another Christian as a source of encouragement in your new life. Congratulations! And welcome to the family.

Chapter 1

1 Chuck Colson, as related by Ken Blanchard in *Insights on Leadership*, ed. Larry C. Spears (New York: John Wiley & Sons, 1998) p. 26
2 J. Oswald Sanders, *Spiritual Leadership* (Chicago: Moody Press, 1967) p. 13.
3 J.F. Baldwin, *The Deadliest Monster* (Eagle Creek, OR: Coffee House, 1998).
4 William James, *The Book of Positive Quotations*, ed. John Cook (Minneapolis: Fairview Press, 1996) p. 294
5 Bernie Miklasz, *Mastermind with a Winning Obsession: Single-minded Demeanor Drives Cowboys Coach* (St. Louis Post-Dispatch, January 28, 1993) p. 1D
6 Max Lucado, *Just Like Jesus* (Nashville, TN: Word Publishing, 1998). p. 166.

Chapter 2

1 J. Oswald Sanders, *Spiritual Leadership* (Chicago: Moody Press, 1967), p. 31.
2 Robert A. Fitton, *Leadership* (Boulder: Westview Press, 1997), p. 163.
3 T.B. Macaulay in *Edinburgh Review*, July 1843.
4 C.S. Lewis, *Christian Reflections* (Grand Rapids: Eerdmans Publishing, 1967) p. 33.
5 Sanders, p. 39.
6 John C. Maxwell, *Leadership 101* (Tulsa: Honor Books, 1994), p. 18.
7 Ralph Waldo Emerson, *The Conduct of Life – Considerations by the way* (1860).
8 Booker T. Washington as quoted in David Wallechinsky, *The Peoples Almanac presents the 20th Century* (Boston: Little, Brown and Company, 1995), p. 6.
9 Albert Schweitzer, to a group of tourists, cited in James B. Simpson, ed., *Simpson's Contemporary Quotations* (New York: Harper Collins, 1997), p. 388.
10 Attributed.
11 Attributed.
12 Blaise Pascal, *Pensees* (New York: Penguin Books, 1986) p. 251.
13 Thomas A. Edison, *Life* (1932) ch. 24
14 G.K. Chesterton, *What's Wrong with the World* (1910) pt. I, ch. 5.
15. Jerry Clower, *Stories from Home*, (University Press of Mississippi, 1992). pp. 43-44.

Chapter 3

1 John C. Maxwell, *Developing the Leader Within You* (Nashville: Thomas Nelson, 1993), p. 131.
2 Gerhard Kittel, *Theological Dictionary of the New Testament*, vol. III (Grand Rapids: WM. B. Eerdmans, 1965), s.v. "Kubernesis," pp. 1035 ff.
3 Texas Bix Bender, *Don't Squat With Yer Spurs On!* (Salt Lake City: Peregrin Smith, 1992), p. 37.
4 William A. Cohen, *The Art of the Leader* (Englewood Cliffs, New Jersey: Prentice Hall, 1990), p. 5.
5 Samuel Logan Brengle, *The Soul-Winner's Secret* (London: Salvation Army, 1918), p. 22.
6 Jamie Clarke and Alan Hobson, *The Power of Passion*, (Calgary, AB: Stewart Publishing, 1997). p. 187.

Chapter 4

1 Lord Acton, letter to Mandell Creighton, April 5, 1887.— *Acton, Essays on Freedom and Power*, ed. Gertrude Himmelfaize, pp. 335-36 (1972).
2 Rudyard Kipling, *Rewards and Fairies*—"IF" (1910) st. 4.
3 Dwight D. Eisenhower, *America's God and Country*, ed. William J. Federer (Coppell: FAME Publishing, 1994) p. 226.
4 Oliver Wendell Holmes Jr., March 8, 1931, Bartlett's p. 645.
5 Joseph Stevens, *Hoover Dam: An American Adventure* (Norman, OK: University of Oklahoma Press, 1988). p. 258

Chapter 5

1 Billy Graham, guest editorial *New York Times*, March 17, 1998, p. A31.
2 Sally Magnuson, *The Flying Scotsman* (New York: Quartet, 1981) p. 40.
3 Booker T. Washington, *Up from Slavery* (1901) (New York: The Modern Library, 1999) p. 11-12
4 Dwight D. Eisenhower, *Great Quotes From Great Leaders*, ed. Peggy Anderson (Lombard: Great Quotations, 1989).
5 Thanks to Jim Little of Grace Community Church in Tyler, Texas for suggesting this comparison.
6 Attributed.
7 Elmer Bendiner, *The Fall of Fortresses* (New York: Putnam, c1980) pp. 138-139
8 William Bross, *America's God and Country*, ed. William J. Federer (Coppell: FAME Publishing, 1994) p. 76.

Chapter 6

1 Thomas Carlyle, *Sartor Resartus* (1833-1834)
2 Peter Marshall, Senate chaplain, prayer offered at the opening of the session, April 18, 1947.—*Prayers Offered by the Chaplain, The Rev. Peter Marshall...1947-1948*, p. 20 (1949). Senate Doc. 80-170.
3 Tim Hansel, *When I Relax I Feel Guilty* (Elgin, IL: David C. Cook, 1979) pp. 146-147
4 J.F. Baldwin, *The Deadliest Monster* (Eagle Creek, OR: Coffee House, 1998), p.28.
5 Attributed.
6 Baldwin, p. 29.
7 Bill Lawerence & Jack Turpin, *Beyond the Bottom Line* (Chicago: Moody Press, 1994) p. 70.
8 Father Theodore Hesburgh as quoted by Ezra Bowen in *Time* Magazine.
9 General Colin L. Powell USA (Ret.), *Austin College Magazine* Summer/Fall 1998, p. 23
10 Billy Graham, *Just As I Am*, (Harpercollins Worldwide, 1997). p. 169.

Chapter 7

1 Viktor E. Frankl, *Man's Search for Meaning* (New York: Simon & Schuster, 1985) p. 85.
2 Chuck Swindoll, *Strengthening Your Grip* (Waco: Word Publishing, 1981) pp. 206-207.
3 Attributed.

Chapter 8

1 Ralph Sockman, *Thoughts on Leadership* (Chicago: Triumph Books, 1995) p. 20.
2 Walter Lippman, *Roosevelt Has Gone* (April 14, 1945)
3 John C. Maxwell, *Leadership 101* (Tulsa: Honor Books, 1994), p. 18.
4 John Bunyan. 1678, *Pilgrims Progress,* pt. II, Shepherd Boy's Song. John Bartlett, Bartlett's Familiar Quotations (Boston: Little, Brown and Company, 1855, 1980), p. 302.
5 William Penn. *Some Fruits of Solitude*, 1693.
6 James Newton, *Uncommon Friends* (San Diego: Harcourt Brace, 1989), p. 19.
7 Plutarch, *The Book of Positive Quotations*, ed. John Cook (Minneapolis: Fairview Press,1996), p. 518.
8 Tom Peters, *The Pursuit of WOW!* (New York: Random House, 1994) p. 31.
9 Aubrey Newman, *Follow Me* (Presidio, CA: Presidio Press, 1981) pp. 176-77.
10 Attributed.
11 Associated Press, February 12, 1991.
12 Walter A. Henrichsen, *Disciple Are Made Not Born* (Colorado Springs, CO: ChariotVictor Publishing, 1974). p. 9-10.

Chapter 9

1 Joe Griffith, *Speaker's Library of Business Stories, Anecdotes and Humor*. Prentice Hall (New Jersey, 1990) p. 12.
2 Attributed.
3 Rosa Parks, *Quiet Strength*, (Grand Rapids: Zondervan, 1995).

Chapter 10

1 William Shakespeare, *Macbeth I*, vii 59.
2 Thomas Paine. *The American Crisis* (December 23, 1776).
3 C.S. Lewis, *The Voyage of the Dawn Treader* (New York: Harper Collins, 1952) p. 231
4 Aleksandr Solzhenitsyn, *The First Circle* (New York, NY: Harper & Row, 1990) p. 3.
5 Paul De Gondi. *Memoirs, Bk. II* (1655-1665)
6 Theodore Roosevelt, speech before the Hamilton Club, Chicago (April 10, 1899).
7 36th Infantry Division Association, 1999.
   http://www.kwanah.com/36division/ps/ps930475.htm: Author unknown.